CALIFORNIA'S MOST NOTORIOUS CRIMES
1900-1950

Margaret LaPlante

Fonthill Media Inc.
www.fonthill.media
office@fonthillmedia.com

First published 2024
Copyright © Margaret LaPlante 2024

ISBN 978-1-62545-142-2

All rights reserved. No part of this publication may be reproduced, stored in a retrieval system or transmitted in any form or by any means, electronic, mechanical, photocopying, recording or otherwise, without prior permission in writing from Fonthill Media Inc.

Typeset in Sabon 10pt on 13.5pt
Printed and bound in England

Contents

Introduction		5
1	The Yacht Bandits	7
2	Charles Drossner	16
3	The Kidnapping of Marion Parker	21
4	Frank Egan and Dr. Nathan Housman	34
5	Thomas and Burmah White	52
6	Floyd Woodward	57
7	Emma LeDoux	60
8	The Mysterious Death of Thelma Todd	65
9	Arthur Eggers	70
10	Louise Peete	74
11	Walburga "Dolly" Oesterreich	81
12	Charles Henry Schwartz	86
13	San Diego Murders	91
14	Juanita "The Duchess" Spinelli	102
15	Escape from Alcatraz	106
16	Albert LeRoy Jones	120
17	The Tom Gray Gang	126
18	The Bombing of the Los Angeles Times Building	129
19	The Pasadena Murder Mystery	133
20	The Thirty Strong Gang	135
Endnotes		140
Bibliography		143

Introduction

Within the pages of this book are some of the crimes that shook the otherwise serene state of California.

"The biggest blow-up in the history of Los Angeles," declared the sheriff of Los Angeles County after learning that three men had been wrongfully convicted as part of a cover up involving high-ranking officials in Los Angeles.

"I wouldn't hurt a hair on her head," said a man who later admitted he murdered his wife and left her headless torso on the Rim of the World Highway. Moments before being executed, he emphatically stated, "I may have shot her, but I never cut her up."

The "most red-handed and brutal murderess ever known in this country," stated the prosecution after the discovery of one murder led to multiple murders.

"Her hair was afire when I looked last," stated a fourteen-year-old boy accused of killing a classmate and setting her house on fire. He made the matter-of-fact statement while being questioned about murdering his neighbor as she was preparing to give him some cookies for a snack.

"I'm tired of running. I'm sick of remorse," stated a man who surrendered to police after nineteen years. The suspect was able to recall minute details of the homicide that only the murderer would know.

"Every cell is identical and every prisoner is given identical treatment, with no exceptions for Capone or anyone else," explained the warden of Alcatraz Federal Penitentiary.

When asked about ordering a hit on one of her own gang members, a woman known as "The Duchess" admitted to the investigators she "wanted it to be a mercy killing, because I kind of liked the boy."

"My heart is filled with gratitude for all my neighbors and friends, who are so nobly sustaining us during this time," stated the man law enforcement referred to as the "kingpin" of gambling operations in Atlanta, Georgia. He started a new life in California under an assumed name, but it was not enough to outrun the long arm of the law that spent twenty years looking for him.

"Either prison beats me or I beat it and I intend to beat it." Those were the words spoken by a nineteen-year-old female on her way to prison after being convicted of a series of robberies committed with her husband, including one on their wedding day.

1
The Yacht Bandit

The customers inside the Western States Bank on South Western Avenue in Los Angeles on December 18, 1923 noticed a young man with his arm in a sling. What no one knew was that the man's arm was not injured; he was simply using the sling to conceal a handgun which he used to quietly rob the bank before walking out the door with $1,000.

The man might have gotten away with the scheme had he not told his friend, Fulton Jacks. Fulton decided to try the gun-in-a-sling trick, but he was promptly arrested. He wasted no time telling the police, "Well, it didn't work this time," before naming his friend, Lloyd Edison Sampsell, age twenty-nine, as the brains behind the operation.

Lloyd soon found himself in handcuffs, which led to a trial where he was found guilty and sentenced to San Quentin prison. Lloyd wiled away his time in prison planning future bank robberies.

After Lloyd was released from prison, a series of bank robberies hit the West Coast. The police in each town where a bank robbery took place would scour the streets looking for their suspect, but always came up empty handed.

During the same time frame, the police in Vancouver, British Columbia, were struggling to apprehend what they dubbed the "phantom bandit." The phantom bandit earned his nickname after entering businesses and homes, helping himself to what he wanted, and then disappearing. This subject also would go to auto dealerships and ask to go for a test drive. Once he drove out to a secluded area, he would leave the auto salesperson chained to a tree before he took off with the stolen car.

In 1929, the Vancouver police believed Lloyd was the "phantom bandit" after piecing together enough details from cases within their district. At the time, they were investigating a case involving the theft of services from Hoffar-Beech Company. The Hoffar-Beech Company provided boat repairs and a customer giving the name "McNab" attempted to pick up his 45-foot yacht without paying the repair bill of $343. The man was with two female companions. Mr. Hoffar tried unsuccessfully to prevent the trio from taking the yacht.

The Vancouver police were busy dealing with five burglaries about the same time the yacht was taken from the repair shop. They placed the blame squarely on the phantom bandit. They sent a telegram to the Los Angeles Police Department requesting a photograph of Lloyd. Once they received the photograph, Lloyd was positively identified by a number of people in Vancouver.

Armed with this information, the police in Vancouver requested the Seattle and Puget Sound Police Departments search their cities for Lloyd, figuring he may have gone to one of those cities after he left Vancouver in the yacht. The police in Vancouver also contacted the San Francisco Police Department and provided them with a possible address where Lloyd might be. They had reason to believe Lloyd shipped an expensive automobile to San Francisco from Vancouver using the name of "L.V. Summers."

Detectives with the San Francisco Police Department were waiting for Lloyd when he arrived in San Francisco. He was accompanied by a female who identified herself as Lloyd's wife, Lydia Summers, and a friend, identified as Ethan Allen McNab, age thirty-two.

Ethan's criminal past included other bank robberies for which he served time in San Quentin prison. Prior to that, Ethan worked as a chauffeur in Los Angeles. Lloyd was the son of a wealthy restaurateur who provided him with an allowance of $250 per month.

The police referred to the interior of Lloyd's apartment in San Francisco as an arsenal. They found high-powered rifles equipped with silencers, shotguns with tear-gas mechanisms, hundreds of rounds of ammunition, and numerous pistols. The detectives located $10,000 in the apartment consisting of cash and checks believed to be from one or more bank robberies.

The San Francisco Police Department quickly seized the yacht, named the *Sovereign*, that was anchored at the exclusive St. Francis Yacht Club in the San Francisco Harbor. They located additional currency, traveler's checks, and bank notes in the yacht, all of which they believed to have been stolen during one or more bank robberies. The U.S. Coast Guard admitted they would not have been able to outrun the yacht due to the potential speed the yacht could travel.

The manager of the Bank of America branch on Dwight Way in Berkeley positively identified Lloyd as the suspect who held up his bank and made off with $18,000. Lloyd was also identified as a suspect in two bank robberies in Los Angeles, and another in San Diego. Law enforcement believed Lloyd was responsible for at least five other bank robberies in the greater Los Angeles area.

Once the suspects were in custody, law enforcement learned that while they had been searching for their bank robbery suspects in each city, the bank robbers, Lloyd and Ethan, had escaped to their yacht after each robbery and headed off into the sunset. From that time forward, they became known as the "yacht bandits."

The charges against Lydia were dropped due to a lack of evidence. Lloyd and Ethan were indicted by the Alameda County grand jury for the bank robbery in Berkeley. They both pled innocent to the bank robbery charge and a trial date was set for two weeks out.

A jury deliberated two hours before finding Lloyd and Ethan guilty of robbing the bank in Berkeley. They were sentenced to fifteen years to life and incarcerated at Folsom prison.

Lydia settled in Sacramento to be close to Lloyd and awaited the birth of their baby. Lydia was the mother to a three-year-old daughter from a previous relationship. She vowed to "stick by Lloyd until he is freed." She described for a reporter the night she was arrested by saying, "I thought we had got into the wrong apartment when we came in and three men rushed forward. I could not believe that the police had any reason to want us. I can hardly believe it yet. Then the jail. I'd never seen a jail before. There was a woman, laughing and screaming, somewhere down the row of cells. I could not sleep, and yet it seemed that I must be dreaming-one of those terrible dreams from which you wake up weeping."[1]

A month later, Lloyd and Ethan went on trial for a bank robbery in Oakland. Employees of the bank described for the jury being forced at gunpoint to lay on the floor of the office while the bank robbers grabbed what they could from the cash drawers. They explained they were then led into the vault while the robbers made off with $10,133. Each of the employees positively identified Lloyd and Ethan, as did witnesses who saw them leave the bank. The jury deliberated for seventeen minutes before returning a verdict of guilty. Lloyd and Ethan received a second term of fifteen years to life imprisonment.

It took the duo less than a year at Folsom prison to come up with an escape plan. When they were not present at the nightly lineup, prison officials began scouring the prison and the prison yard looking for them.

The prison officials believed the men had not been able to leave the prison grounds, but a thorough search of the prison did not reveal anything. They blasted tear gas everywhere they thought the men might be able to hide within the prison. When that failed, they requested an architect to respond to the prison with the original blueprints of the entire prison. They studied the blueprints, looking for any openings the men could hide in.

The prison warden paid a visit to Lydia who was living in Sacramento with her newborn baby and her daughter. Lydia denied having any knowledge of an escape plan. She told the prison warden that she was planning to divorce Lloyd, explaining: "I think divorce would be best, even though I still love him dearly. There are children to think of, you know." Law enforcement posted an officer at Lydia's house in the event Lloyd tried to contact her.

As it turned out, the men never left the prison grounds. They were located hiding underneath the blacksmith shop. Prison officials learned a fellow inmate had concealed them by covering up the small space they were hiding in. Lloyd and Ethan had planned to stay in the hole briefly until they were able to make their getaway, but they ended up being there for 147 hours. Although the tear gas never reached them in their hiding place, the food and water they hid in the hole ran out before they had a chance to escape. Both men were placed in isolation.

Less than one year later, two men were arrested for attempting to smuggle guns into Folsom prison to aid Lloyd and Ethan's next attempt at escaping. The weapons consisted of three loaded pistols and sixty-six rounds of ammunition that were concealed in a container of nails that was delivered to the prison. James Palese and Emil Colson were arrested for their involvement in smuggling firearms into the prison. A search of James' house revealed what the officials referred to as a "veritable arsenal" consisting of sawed-off shotguns, pistols, tear gas guns, and ammunition.

During the trial of James and Emil, testimony revealed that James repeatedly attempted to purchase a submachine gun but was turned down due to laws in place at the time. The court also learned Lloyd and Ethan had attempted to smuggle 1,000,000 rounds of ammunition and 500 revolvers into Mexico prior to their arrest and being sent to prison. During the trial, Emil confessed that Lloyd and Ethan promised to include his brother, Marvin Colson, in their escape plan, if Emil would supply the firearms to help them escape from Folsom prison. The charges against James and Emil were dropped after Emil repudiated his confession. Emil was later convicted of perjury.

Months later, prison guards discovered that a small hole had been drilled in Lloyd's cell door. Lloyd admitted to the warden that he was responsible for drilling the hole but refused to say how he had acquired the drill. Once the prison officials learned Lloyd, Ethan, and another inmate, Thomas Fleming, were planning to escape, they transferred Ethan to San Quentin prison. Lloyd and Thomas were placed in solitary confinement.

Ethan's transfer to San Quentin did not curtail his desire to escape the prison walls. Ethan and three other inmates attempted to overpower two guards using makeshift firearms they had fashioned out of metal and shells. As the four inmates made their bid for freedom, Ethan's makeshift weapon fired, killing an inmate who was not involved in the escape plot. Ethan managed to overpower one guard and steal his uniform before another guard shot at the four escapees, none of whom were injured. Ethan and his accomplices were overtaken and placed in solitary confinement. Two of the escapees were acquitted. Ethan and the other escapee were hanged for the murder of the inmate during their escape attempt.

Lloyd's next attempt at escaping from Folsom prison included Emil's brother, Marvin Colson. Marvin was serving a life sentence for murder. Lloyd and Marvin came up with an escape plan wherein they would force their way into the prison office using guns they made from various bits and pieces of metal they had saved over time. Their plan was to have the administrative staff telephone the warden and ask him to respond to the office. Their plan fell apart when the staff called the warden, who sensed something was wrong. He summoned prison guards to surround the office building. Lloyd realized their plan had failed and he surrendered. Marvin committed suicide using his homemade gun rather than surrendering.

Each passing year brought a new escape plan for Lloyd. In 1936, he was named the ringleader of a plan that involved arranging for four firearms and 100 rounds of ammunition to be left in a can and buried in the dirt along the railroad track just outside of the prison. An inmate trusty who was scheduled to be released the following week was caught bringing the guns into the prison while working on the railroad. One prison official summed up Lloyd's many attempts at escaping by saying, "Sampsell is a model prisoner, until he conceives one of his escape ideas. Then he's a bad fellow. He never is involved in the petty trouble at the prison."

Due to Lloyd's many attempts at escaping, he spent most of his time in solitary confinement. When he was finally released from solitary confinement, Warden Clyde Plummer told the media: "Today Sampsell came to me and said, 'Warden, I don't know how to thank you. Words can't describe my true feelings. I promise you there will be no more trouble from me or my friends in this prison.'" The warden went onto explain to the media: "I feel that Sampsell wasn't placed in solitary confinement for what he had done-the officials were afraid of what he might do."

Lloyd's next attempts at leaving Folsom prison were through requesting to be paroled, but his requests were denied. He was assigned to a prison work farm in Yolo County.

In 1943, California Governor Warren told the media: "There cannot possibly be any excuse for this situation, because everyone who knows anything about criminals in California knows there isn't a more desperate or more murderous fellow than Lloyd Sampsell. This is the most outrageous thing that I have ever heard of in prison management-to permit a murderous convict such as Sampsell to have the liberty that he has been given. It shows a total irresponsibility on the part of the warden and an absolute disregard for the safety of the public."[2]

The governor spoke those words after learning Lloyd had been leaving the prison work farm and visiting his girlfriend in San Francisco. Lloyd defended the visits saying he always gave a prison guard the phone number where he could be reached. Warden Plummer stated: "It seems the camp has been a little loose at times." The female Lloyd had been visiting explained she visited Lloyd in prison after reading a poem he had written. She went onto say she had known Lloyd "in my other life" and "I thought I could save him from himself."

The following week, Governor Warren told the Associated Press: "Plummer was suspended by the board last Sunday when it was learned Sampsell, who was permitted to leave the prison and work with other convicts in a harvest camp near Davis, Yolo County, made frequent trips from the camp including visits to a woman friend in San Francisco." The governor explained: "Sampsell as head of the print shop for more than three years had more or less the run of the prison after Plummer became warden."[3] Governor Warren added that he closed the harvest camp program after learning of Sampsell's departures and fired the guard in charge of the program. Warden Plummer resigned, and the state legislature requested that the prison system be studied in depth.

After five escape attempts, seven unsuccessful bids for parole, and eighteen years behind bars, Lloyd was paroled on September 16, 1947. The parole board decided Lloyd should be "given a chance to make good," citing that he had been a "model prisoner" in recent years. Lloyd was scheduled to take a job at a printing facility in Los Angeles.

Six months later, the FBI was searching for Lloyd who had decidedly not made good. This time he was wanted for murder and robbery. On March 27, 1948, Lloyd, Ben Richardson, and William Burke held up the Seaboard Finance Corporation in San Diego. During the robbery, a customer, Arthur Smith, age fifty-five, of Chula Vista, was shot and killed. Chula Vista Police Officer Harley Cook who was working as a special investigator for the Seaboard Finance Company was wounded in the shootout.

William Burke was arrested in Santa Barbara. He adamantly denied being involved in the robbery. Days later, he admitted to being the lookout and getaway driver, saying he only received $35.

Ben turned himself in to the authorities in Billings, Montana, saying his conscience compelled him to do so. He was charged with murder, intent to commit murder, robbery, and assault with a deadly weapon. Ben told the authorities Lloyd was the one who received the bulk of the robbery proceeds. The day before Ben was scheduled to go on trial, he pled guilty to second-degree murder and was sentenced to five years in prison. The other charges were dismissed in exchange for the guilty plea.

While the police were actively looking for Lloyd for the murder and robbery, he was identified in two additional robberies. Both robberies occurred at other branches of the Seaboard Finance Company. However, at the Inglewood branch, Lloyd left empty handed after none of the employees could open the safe.

A short time later, Lloyd walked into the Anglo California National Bank and handed the teller a note which read: "Have a gun ... two buddies. Give me $1500 in bills ... Don't say or turn in alarm for five minutes. The other two are still here." He left with $719.

There were four bank robberies in San Francisco in under four weeks. Some of the victims positively identified Lloyd as the suspect, while others were not sure. Lloyd was also a suspect in the $1,120 robbery of the Fresno Loan and Thrift Company, as well as a bank robbery in Los Angeles.

After nearly a year of hunting down Lloyd, the FBI placed him on their "Most Wanted List." An employee with Trans World Airlines, Dale Jensen, saw the most wanted list the day before a man came up to him and asked for details about a particular flight. Dale answered the man's questions, and the man left the area, but Dale was bothered by the man's resemblance to one of the men on the most wanted list. Dale alerted Los Angeles Police Officer Henry Wild, who was working at the Los Angeles airport.

Officer Wild boarded the plane that was warming up and about to take off. Officer Wild located Lloyd on the plane and requested he step to the back of the plane. Officer Wild questioned Lloyd but ultimately let him get back in his seat and leave on the plane because the FBI's most wanted list showed that Lloyd had brown eyes and the man standing before him had blue eyes.

Nevertheless, Officer Wild had a feeling that something was not quite right. He contacted the FBI, and they were waiting for the plane to touch down at the Sky Harbor Airport in Phoenix. The FBI made arrangements with the Phoenix Police Department who provided five detectives to assist with the arrest. Lloyd was traveling under the name of H. P. Shaw and was on his way to Kansas City, Missouri. Lloyd did not show any surprise when he was surrounded by law enforcement. He was carrying a loaded firearm and $7,800 at the time of his arrest. Lloyd admitted to Special Agent Murphy: "I have been expecting something like this. I was hot and I knew they would be on the lookout for me."

Once Lloyd was at the Phoenix Federal Building, he admitted to FBI Agent H. M. Clegg that he robbed a Bank of America in Los Angeles the day before his arrest. That robbery netted him $8,700 and involved holding up a car salesperson at gunpoint and stealing a car minutes before he robbed the bank. Lloyd denied being involved in the robbery at the Seaboard Finance Company in San Diego where Arthur Smith was killed. Lloyd told FBI Agent H. M. Clegg he blamed a "so-called reform school" for his criminal career, adding, "there is no such thing as a reform school."

Lloyd was held without bail while the paperwork was sent from California. Lloyd waived extradition and was returned to California. He pled innocent to the charge of murder, attempted murder, and armed robbery.

Lloyd's trial began on May 17, 1949 with Superior Court Judge William Glen presiding. The state of California was represented by Don Keller. Lloyd was represented by defense attorney Robert Barbour. The defense admitted to the all-female jury that although Lloyd was present at the bank robbery, he was not responsible for killing Arthur and wounding Officer Cook.

The manager of Seaboard Finance Company, Robert Runyon, took the witness stand and identified Lloyd as the bank robber who ordered him at gunpoint to open the bank's safe and stole $3,451. Robert explained to the jury that Arthur Smith was a customer in the bank at the time of the robbery, and he attempted to stop Lloyd and his partners as they exited the building. Robert went into detail about Lloyd firing his gun three times and, in doing so, killing Arthur and wounding Officer Cook. Four other employees of the Seaboard Finance Company took the witness stand and identified Lloyd as the bank robber.

The defense called Lloyd's partner in the robbery at the Seaboard Finance Company, Ben Richardson, to the witness stand. It was his testimony that Lloyd was the one who fired the gun three times.

Lloyd took the witness stand and admitted he fired his gun which resulted in the death of Arthur and the wounding of Officer Cook. He told the jury: "It happened just like most of the witnesses said." Lloyd quickly added: "I had no conscious remembrance of firing the shots." Lloyd's defense attorney requested that Lloyd be allowed to undergo mental tests, claiming that Lloyd's inability to remember was due to psycho-motor-epilepsy. The request was granted but the doctors declared Lloyd to be "perfectly normal."

The jury found Lloyd guilty of first-degree murder, attempted murder, armed robbery, and assault. The jury did not recommend leniency, meaning Lloyd would be executed. Superior Court Judge Glen sentenced Lloyd to die in the gas chamber at San Quentin prison. Later that year, Lloyd mailed a Christmas card to the judge with a handwritten note that stated, "Joy and happiness for Christmas and the New Year."

Lloyd was scheduled to be executed on July 21, 1950. Two days before Lloyd was to die in the gas chamber, a stay of execution was granted. The Ninth Circuit Court of Appeals denied his appeal. The U.S. Supreme Court rejected his appeal, and a new execution date was set for April 25, 1952.

As the date of his execution loomed, Lloyd reflected on his life when he was interviewed by the media. He began by saying:

> Twenty-five years and more in prison, four years of it in solitary. It makes a guy want to talk. To get it out of his system.
>
> Look, here's something I've never told anyone. I've got a son. He's six foot three, 170 pounds. He's married, got two kids. He's in the service, overseas right now. A good boy. So I've left something good. You can't say my life was wasted.

When questioned about the looming execution, Lloyd said: "I got time. I got faith in this writ. I figure they sliced the law a little thin in San Diego." Lloyd explained: "They told the jury they could go ahead and find me guilty of first-degree murder without worrying about having my death on their conscience because there was an automatic appeal to the supreme court. He sort of left them off the moral hook. That wasn't right."[4]

The day prior to Lloyd's execution, his parents traveled from Los Angeles to visit him for the last time. Later that evening, Lloyd spoke to two chaplains and reminisced with prison guards. His last dinner consisted of chicken and a berry pie. His final breakfast was oatmeal, orange juice, and coffee. Lloyd questioned why anyone would be interested in knowing what he ate for his final meal, saying, "I don't know why this should bother me but I don't know why people should be interested in what the condemned man ate for breakfast."

The man dubbed the "Yacht Bandit" was executed on April 25, 1952 at 10:13 a.m. He was fifty-two years old and had spent more than half of his life behind bars.

2
Charles Drossner

Charles could be considered a world traveler, having visited Japan, Mexico, Algeria, Spain, Italy, Holland, Great Britain, Belgium, Argentina, Germany, France, and Austria. The difference between Charles and other global travelers was that Charles spent time in jails in each of these countries.

Charles was born in 1890 in San Francisco. Growing up he became fluent in English, German, French, Spanish, and Russian. His first foray into crime was writing bad checks. In 1907, Charles was sent to Preston Reformatory in Ione, California, for that crime. His parents sent him to Japan after he was released, hoping he would change his ways, but he was soon in trouble with the authorities in Japan on fraud charges. Charles returned to the United States, but his crimes continued.

Charles served in the French Foreign Legion during World War I. Soon after the war ended, Charles was arrested for unlawfully wearing the uniform of a lieutenant of the French Army. Charles was incensed at the time of his arrest, saying: "I am going to get a square break out of this. Here I went to France and got a finger shot off and a dozen shrapnel wounds in the head; got my citations for bravery and a lieutenancy, as well as an honorable discharge, and now here I am in the county jail, a prisoner and being persecuted."

Charles expanded by saying:

> My captain, Lehagre, had penetrated the German trenches and was wounded. I went in after him and picked him up. On the way back he was hit and killed in my arms. The first finger of my left hand was shot away. I was in the hospital eleven months and was discharged on March 29, 1916, my commission being cancelled at that time on account of my wounds. After my return to New York I registered for the draft and afterwards I tried to get into the tank corps, but was turned down on account of wounds.[1]

Charles said Captain Lehagre promoted him to lieutenant when he carried him out of the trench. He said he was awarded a bravery citation for his actions. Some of the men who served with Charles had a different version of the story. They did not believe Charles was ever promoted to lieutenant nor was he ever awarded any citations. Charles also claimed to have an engineering degree from Stanford University, but others said Charles left the university prior to graduating.

While serving during World War I, Charles was court-martialed and sentenced to two years for desertion. Charles admitted he left the French Foreign Legion, but said it was only so he could re-enlist. While in France, Charles married Madeline Bory in Livry.

While living in France after the war, Charles was arrested for writing a fraudulent check. Charles ended up being expelled from France and told never to return.

In 1918, Charles was wanted in Baltimore, Maryland, for writing two fraudulent checks. The police in Chicago, Illinois, were also looking for Charles on similar charges. Charles was arrested but a female friend bailed him out, explaining that even though she had just met him, she believed in him. Once free on bail, Charles told the media he had "been entertained by many of the finest people in Chicago." Charles was quick to mention having been to Judge Pam's house. Upon learning of this, Judge Pam immediately contacted the media and emphasized that Charles had never been to his house.

Once back in San Francisco, Charles told reporters he received honors from France, Belgium, England, and Russia for bringing down eleven German planes. He expanded by saying that the Germans held him as a prisoner of war, but he managed to escape from their clutches. Soon after, Charles was arrested in San Francisco for obtaining money under false pretenses and sentenced to six months in jail.

After being released from jail, Charles filed for divorce from Madeline, citing her adultery. While he was waiting for the divorce to be granted, Charles was arrested in Los Angeles for fraudulent checks. Charles insisted the checks were simply a "mistake" and that he would pay for the bad checks. Charles explained the accounting error by saying he was a cinema director and was headed to Mexico for filming.

After serving time in California, Charles was back in France but was soon arrested in Bayonne, France, for writing fraudulent checks. At that time, he was using the alias of Douglas Campbell. He was sent to jail for the fraudulent checks and also for failing to obey the order from years before that he never return to France, having been previously expelled from the country.

In 1924, Charles was sentenced to seven months in prison in Rome on a charge of swindling. He used the alias Jose de Braganca while in Rome. After serving time in Rome, Charles was arrested in Paris for forgery. He also was arrested in Holland for defrauding an innkeeper.

The next time Charles turned up he was in Vienna, claiming to be Prince de Braca of Portugal. He carried a passport showing he was Prince de Braca of

Portugal. He was arrested for fraudulent checks, unpaid bills, and impersonating an officer. Once he was in custody, he gave the fictious name of Chester Smith. The State Department was asked to investigate the real identity of the inmate. They were able to quickly identify the prisoner as Charles Drossner.

After returning to the United States, Charles was arrested in New York and charged with grand larceny. The charges were later dropped for lack of evidence. It was not long before Charles was charged with a new case of forgery, but that case was reduced to petit larceny.

Charles was ousted from the Cuba Good Will Committee after it was determined he had used the title for "private interest." The investigation revealed Charles had used his title to obtain goods and currency with no intention of paying for the goods.

In 1932, Charles was featured in a bulletin that the FBI sent to all police chiefs in the United States. Charles was recognized by law enforcement and was arrested in Santa Monica for charges stemming from Wisconsin. At the time of his arrest, he was wanted in San Francisco, Los Angeles, San Diego, New York, Utah, and Colorado.

Charles was extradited to Wisconsin where the Milwaukee police were waiting for him. A trial was held with many witnesses taking the stand and describing for the jury how Charles had conned them out of money. Some of the charges were for writing fraudulent checks. Other charges were for ordering merchandise without the intention of paying for the goods. The jury heard from several police officers who testified that Charles used aliases, including L. C. Young, S. A. Soto, Max Schwartz, P. G. Mendoza, Pablo Soto, P. C. Adler, Leon D. Spitzer, S. C. Kaufman, Charles Deschamps, Chester Smith, and Joe Braganca.

The jury deliberated for nearly four hours before finding Charles guilty of writing a bad check in the amount of $75 and sentenced him to one to five years in the Waupun prison for fraud. Other charges for swindling businesses out of $300 were not brought to trial. Charles was booked into the Waupun prison as prisoner number 20652. His fingerprints were sent to the Division of Investigation at the Department of Justice in Washington, D.C. Charles became one of the first criminals to have his fingerprints sent to foreign countries. In Charles' case, the authorities discovered he was wanted in other countries for forgery and fraud. This case became one of the first for cooperation and sharing of information on an international basis.

When New Scotland Yard received Charles' fingerprints, they were able to tie him to forgery charges in Great Britain. Further investigation showed that Charles had been sentenced to servitude for life in prison in Devil's Island in France and fined 3,000 francs for forgery. Law enforcement in Belgium also reported Charles was wanted there for forgery. In Belgium, Charles had used aliases to include Douglas Campbelle, Jose Brancanza, Jose Carlos Branzanca, Daniel Chester, and Vincent Montoya.

When interviewed by reporters, Deputy Warden Taft of the Waupun prison said:

> We put no stock in his denials. He is surely one of the most clever criminals in my 32 years here. He could well pass for anything, a broker, a scholar, a banker. There is something impressive, something imposing about him.
>
> We are keeping him under careful surveillance. He has a job here. Of course, we would never permit a man with such a record to go to one of our model farms or to one of our model camps. He will be kept within the prison walls until it is time for his release. We're taking no chances with a man of his intelligence.[2]

Once the French Embassy learned Charles was in the United States, they requested he be returned to France and Devil's Island. The governor of Wisconsin, A. G. Schmedeman, assigned the state attorney general to investigate the extradition request. The French Embassy held that Charles passed fraudulent national defense bonds in the amount of $140,000. The state attorney general advised that Charles be extradited to France. Before that could happen, Charles requested a pardon from the governor of Wisconsin, citing his innocence. In his request for a pardon, Charles wrote that he had never been in the state of Wisconsin prior to being "brought in by police on erroneous identification." The pardon was not granted, and it was decided that Charles would finish his prison sentence in Wisconsin before being sent to France to serve his life sentence at Devil's Island.

The following year, Charles once again requested a pardon from the governor. This time the pardon was granted and on January 4, 1935, Charles was released from the state prison but was arrested by French authorities as he walked through the front gate of the prison. He was held at the Milwaukee jail to await the outcome of the extradition to Devil's Island. While waiting for a decision, Charles went on a hunger strike at the jail, stating he would not eat until his "citizens" and "constitutional" rights were restored. The jail staff reported that Charles ate his food every day. In response, Charles' attorney said Charles' fellow inmates were the ones who were eating Charles' food.

Meanwhile Charles' supporters who called themselves the "National Drossner Defense Committee" held a series of public meetings to garner support for Charles' fight against extradition to France.

Through his attorneys, Charles continued to fight extradition to France. The battle went all the way to the United States Commissioner. Charles' attorneys presented documents showing he was in the United States when the crimes in France occurred. A handwriting expert, John Tyrell, informed the court he was not able to make a determination based on the photocopies of the documents he was provided. Charles' attorneys explained that the original documents were not available. Another handwriting expert, H. A. Rounds, identified Charles' handwriting as that of "Vincente Montoya" who signed the fraudulent documents.

Leon Drolet, an attorney for the French government, presented a book (*American Fighters in the Foreign Legion—1914 to 1918*) written by Paul Ayres Rockwell. In the book, the author wrote that Charles' injury to his hand was self-inflicted in order to avoid combat. In response, Charles acknowledged he knew the author from their time serving in the French Foreign Legion, but emphasized the author's take on the situation was "pure fabrication."

As the battle came to a conclusion, Federal Judge F. A. Geiger denied Charles' plea for a writ of *habeas corpus*. Charles last chance at freedom lay with Secretary of State Cordell Hull. After studying the case, Secretary of State Hull denied the French government their extradition and Charles walked out of the Milwaukee jail a free man on January 22, 1935. Charles told reporters, "I was so happy when I got out of jail and my heart was beating so fast I had to stop five times while walking five blocks. It doesn't seem a reality yet." Charles said he was not sure of his future plans but added that he planned to return to California.

Charles did return to California, and it was not long before he was arrested for a fraudulent check. He was convicted and served time in Folsom prison. He was released from prison and was next wanted in New Orleans. He was indicted for passing $2,100 in bad checks in New Orleans but skipped bond and fled to Mexico. At the time, Charles was also wanted in Missouri. The FBI placed Charles on their Most Wanted List.

On September 22, 1949, Charles was arrested in Laredo, Texas. The FBI was informed that Charles had been kicked out of Mexico after attempting to defraud the Mexican government. They were waiting for him at the International Bridge as he tried to cross into the United States.

Charles was arraigned before a U.S. Commissioner all the while denying his true identity. He continually told the court his name was Thomas Rogers. Charles finally admitted his true identity and pled innocent. Charles was convicted and once again returned to prison, this time for life.

3

The Kidnapping of Marion Parker

On December 16, 1927, Mary Holt was teaching a class at Mount Vernon Junior High School when a man approached her and asked to take twelve-year-old Marion Parker out of school for the day. He explained that Marion's father, Perry Parker, was in the hospital and he wanted to see Marion. Mary allowed the man to take Marion out of school, but she wondered why the man only asked for Marion, and not both Marion and her twin sister, Marjorie.

Two hours later, Perry received a telegram that read: "Do positively nothing until you receive the special delivery letter." Perry immediately contacted the police. The next telegram arrived a few hours later and read: "Marion secure. Use good judgment. Interference with my plans dangerous." Each of the telegrams was signed, "The Fox."

The next day, a special delivery package arrived at the Parkers' home. A letter in a child's handwriting read, "I think I'll die if I have to be like this much longer." Later that day a man calling himself "The Fox" phoned the Parkers' house and gave Perry seventy-two hours to pay $1,500 in ransom.

The drop of the ransom did not go as planned when the kidnapper spotted two detective cars following Perry's car. The next morning, Perry received another letter. In the letter, the kidnapper wrote he was aware of the detectives following him the previous day. The letter read:

> Today is the last day. If by 8 p.m. you have not received my telephone call then hold a quiet funeral service at your cemetery without the body-on Sunday the 18th. Only God knows where the body of Marion Parker would rest in this event; not much effort is needed to take her life. She may pass out before 8 p.m. So I could not afford to call you and ask for your $1500 for a lifeless mass of flesh.[1]

Later that day, Perry received a telephone call from the kidnapper admonishing him for bringing the police to the previous ransom drop. Arrangements were made for another ransom drop. Perry arrived at the designated spot and handed over $1,500 to a man shielded from the light on a dark street. The kidnapper said he would leave Marion down the street.

Perry rushed down the street only to discover his daughter had been murdered. Marion's head and torso were all that were there. Marion's coat was wrapped around the torso and there was a towel with the torso. The towel was embroidered with the words, "Bellevue Arms Apartments." The police rushed to the apartment complex, but the kidnapper was nowhere in sight. In speaking to the apartment manager, the detectives learned a man by the name of "Donald Evans" rented the apartment. When the detectives inspected the apartment, they found half of a Brazil nut. The detectives had already discovered Brazil nuts in Marion's coat pocket. The apartment manager was able to give the detectives a description of "Donald's" vehicle. The description matched the vehicle the kidnapper drove, right down to the missing doorhandle.

Police were called in from surrounding areas to assist in searching for the kidnapper. The shocked community quickly raised $100,000 for a reward. Crowds gathered in front of the Parkers' home, in front of the courthouse, and in front of the police department. They were very vocal in demanding the police find the person responsible.

Later that night, a letter signed "The Fox" threatened to murder Marion's twin sister, Marjorie. The following day, five additional body parts wrapped in newspaper were located in Elysian Park. An examination of the body parts proved they belonged to Marion. Further investigation revealed Marion had been poisoned prior to being murdered.

The police arrested a dozen subjects within a short time. However, after further investigation, the subjects were released from custody. The investigation led the detectives to a seventeen-year-old male by the name of William "Edward" Hickman. Edward was born on February 1, 1910 in Logan County, Arkansas. The family moved to Kansas City where Edward attended school. Edward moved to California at the beginning of 1927. His mother and fifteen-year-old sister, Mary, followed him to California.

The police located the car they believed the kidnapper drove, abandoned in a parking structure in Los Angeles. The police learned the car had been reported stolen in Kansas City the week prior to the kidnapping.

Chief Cline told the media: "We have irrefutable evidence that Hickman is the murderer of Marion Parker. All officers have been ordered to report back on duty and the greatest manhunt in the history of the southwest is swinging into action to apprehend him."

Chief Cline was referring to their ability to compare fingerprints on the special delivery package, the towel, and the vehicle to Edward by using the Bertillon method. Alphonse Bertillon was a police officer in France when he began studying biometrics. In the late 1800s, Alphonse created an identification system that used photography and measurements. He placed the identifiers on file cards. His file cards numbered in the hundreds of thousands. His system was used by police agencies throughout the world prior to fingerprinting comparison methods and computer models eased the identification system.

The investigation revealed that Edward had been employed for a brief time as a messenger for the First National Bank in Los Angeles where Perry worked. During that time frame, Edward was arrested for writing fraudulent checks in the amount of $200. Shortly after Edward's arrest, his mother and sister moved back to Kansas City. Edward was convicted but was released on probation over the objections of Perry who appeared before the court and spoke out against Edward not being sent to jail.

Edward's mugshots taken at the time of his arrest were duplicated by the photography staff at the police department. Local newspapers allowed the police to use their darkrooms to make additional copies of the arrest photograph. Newspapers across the country carried the news of the murder of Marion Parker and the photograph of the suspect.

Mary Holt, who allowed Edward to leave with Marion, identified him by the photograph as the man who left the school with Marion. Employees at the Padre Hotel also identified Edward's photograph as the male they turned away at 1 a.m. on the day of the murder. The employees explained they told the male they would not allow him to stay at the hotel because he did not have any luggage which made them suspicious. They told the detectives the male refused to leave the lobby of the hotel and claimed he had "served time and was a tough guy."

The detectives contacted Edward's mother, Eva, in Kansas City who informed them she had not heard from Edward. When the police informed her that they needed to speak to Edward regarding a kidnapping and murder, Eva became distraught and cried out: "It's all a very, very bad mistake. It is impossible that Edward could have done such a thing. It's terrible—a terrible mistake. My boy would never have done a thing like that. The only trouble he was ever in, was in the bank at Los Angeles, and he was paroled for that." Edward's mother stressed that Edward attended church and Sunday school and had been a good student. Eva gave the detectives a letter Edward wrote to her that was postmarked in Chicago two months prior to the murder. The letter read:

Dear mother:
I thought I would drop you a few lines and let you know where I am. Don't answer this, though, because I don't expect to be at this hotel but a few days. Anyway, you don't need to write me anything.
 Chicago is really a big city. It is nothing like any city I have seen yet.
 Guess you would like to know that I am an usher at the Oriental theater? Am feeling fine and living within my income. Will write you again in two or three weeks.[2]

The detectives notified the police in Kansas City in case Edward attempted to contact his mother. They also notified the police in Arkansas and Oklahoma in the event Edward tried to contact his relatives there.

The manager of the Oriental theater denied that Edward had ever worked at the theater. He explained: "If he ever worked here it was under another name."

Tips poured into the police department which sent officers scrambling to follow up on each tip. Telegrams were sent out nationwide for all police agencies to be on the lookout for Edward. When the investigators learned Edward may have purchased a motorcycle in California, every state traffic officer in California was given orders to stop every motorcycle to see if Edward was the driver.

Frank Peck notified the police that he was the victim of a carjacking, and he believed Edward was responsible. Frank reported he took his wife to a grocery store in Hollywood and while she was inside the store, a male suddenly appeared and got in the passenger seat. The male demanded that Frank drive around the block. Once they were away from the store, the male demanded that Frank hand over his cash and exit the car. The male then drove off with Frank's green Hudson automobile.

Edward's mother requested that a family friend, Colonel Charles Edwards, put an announcement over all radio stations asking Edward to surrender. She later told the media: "I will hear from Edward if he possibly can get word home. He will let me know and when he does Colonel Edwards will assist him."

Edward's parents had divorced when he was a child. His father, Thomas Hickman, remarried and was living in Texas when Edward was being sought. Thomas operated a steam shovel for the Southern Pacific Railway. Through his tears, Thomas told the media:

> If I knew where my son was and could get my hands on him I'd tear him from limb to limb. I would rather be deep in the fires of hell than to have heaped upon me the thought that a boy of mine could be guilty of such a crime. It is hard for me to believe he did it. It is so unlike him.

Thomas recalled: "Why, Edward was not abnormal, at least I never noticed anything strange about him. He always was a leader among kids in school and appeared pretty bright. I can't believe he was vicious or a moron. I just can't think that."[3]

A tip came in saying that Edward was in Seattle, Washington. Shopkeeper George Willoughby told the police Edward came into the store he owned in Seattle. Edward, he said, asked to see a pair of gloves. When shown a pair of gloves, Edward immediately put the gloves on and asked to see some clothing. He quickly selected some items and said, "Wrap it up." Edward paid with a $20 gold certificate note. After Edward left, George was bothered by the thought he had seen the customer somewhere before. As he continued to think about it, he remembered the photograph of Edward in the newspaper.

Later the shopkeeper told reporters: "I opened the till and there was the $20 bill. It was a gold certificate note. I called police headquarters in a hurry and found out that it was one of the ransom notes." George recalled: "He seemed like he was in a hurry to get Christmas shopping done. I was busy with a crowd of customers and was in such a rush that I did not have time to connect the bill with the kidnapping before the man had left the store."[4]

Every police officer in the Seattle area was called in to assist with locating Edward. The city went into martial law, with squads of police placed strategically throughout the city. Police officers were placed at every bridge and every road that led in and out of Seattle. All of the docks and train depots were monitored. Police officers checked every hotel in the city. Motorcycle officers stopped every automobile looking for Edward. Rush-hour traffic was backed up for miles as the police checked every vehicle on the road and examined the identification of every individual in every car. Every city and town in Washington were notified to be on the lookout for Edward. Police officers throughout Washington set up patrols watching for the green Hudson sedan that Edward was supposed to be driving. Thousands of phone calls poured into police stations throughout the state with people reporting sightings of Edward.

Seattle Police Detective Captain William Kent told the media:

He may still be hiding in Seattle in some spot we have missed. If so, he will be captured within a short time, because no corner is being overlooked. It is impossible for a youth hunted like Hickman to escape. Almost everyone in the state has seen his pictures by now. He is, I believe, entirely on his own resources and will undoubtedly walk into some trap.[5]

Despite all of the police presence, Edward managed to elude the officers and drive to Portland, Oregon. A gas station attendant, Fred King, notified the police that Edward refueled the green Hudson in Portland and was heading towards Pendleton, Oregon, at 6:30 a.m. The police in Seattle and Portland broadcast a description of the green Hudson sedan Edward was driving to cities and towns throughout Washington and Oregon. Law enforcement agencies in Pendleton and Umatilla County brought in their off-duty officers to assist in case Edward did enter their jurisdiction.

The nationwide hunt for Edward came to a conclusion on December 22, 1927 in the small town of Echo, Oregon. Pendleton (Oregon) Chief of Police Thomas Gurdane and Oregon State Police Officer Buck Lieuallen were waiting for the green sedan. As the sedan slowed down for a curve on the road, the officers met the sedan with their guns drawn.

Edward and his two companions surrendered without any problem. Edward told the police he had picked up the other two men while driving through The Dalles after leaving Portland. The men were identified as Bill and Jack Merrill. They were armed with weapons but offered no resistance. The brothers were booked into the Umatilla County jail until it was determined their only association with Edward was that he picked them up while they were hitchhiking. The brothers were released from custody.

Edward was booked into the Umatilla County jail. He had $1,400 in gold certificates in his pocket when he was arrested. The serial numbers matched those of the ransom money. Edward admitted to kidnapping Marion but denied killing her saying, "Some fiend killed her. I know who he is," but refused to name the person. Edward continually stated, "I did not kill her." Edward adamantly denied ever being in the apartment where the police believed Marion was murdered. When questioned about his motive, Edward stated, "I did it because I wanted the money to pay my way through college." Although Edward continued to deny killing Marion, he did concede she was strangled with a wire, which caused her death. He further stated that chloroform was never used.

At one point, Edward blurted out, "Andrew Cramer is the man who killed her!" He elaborated and said he and Cramer planned to meet up at the Harris Hotel in San Francisco and split the ransom money. Another time Edward mentioned a female accomplice. Captain William Bright pointed out that the notes that Edward admitted writing never mentioned anyone else was involved. Captain Bright emphasized:

> Hickman said the Parker girl was not killed in the Bellevue Arms Apartment House. We know that she was killed there. If his statement is wrong in that, it is discredited in other details. If this was not a one-man job, why did Hickman have on his person $1400 of the $1500 he collected from the father? If there had been partners, there would have been a split of the money before the trio separated. Hickman did not leave Los Angeles until 24 hours after the body had been delivered and the ransom collected. The fact has been established through the report of the owner of the stolen green Hudson car.[6]

The police officers who were stationed outside the Parkers' house were informed of Edward's arrest. One of the officers shared the news with Marion's father. Upon learning of Edward's capture, Perry told the reporters, "I'm glad, very glad that Hickman has been captured. This strain has been terrible, and I only hope there is no mistake."

Back at the Los Angeles Police Station, cheers were heard throughout the building when Chief of Detectives Herman Cline got word from Oregon and shouted, "We've got him!" to everyone in the building. He made arrangements for a grand jury to convene the following day to formally charge Edward with kidnapping and murder. He also made arrangements to travel to Oregon with District Attorney Asa

Keyes to transport Edward back to Los Angeles. Chief Cline told the media that the travel arrangements would be kept a secret in order to avoid any mob violence. The extradition papers were drawn up and flown by airplane to Oregon.

A biting wind and light snowstorm did not damper the enthusiasm of the residents of Pendleton when news of the arrest of one of the most wanted criminals in America swept through the town. Chief Gurdane felt personally responsible that the most hated man in America did not fall victim to renegade violence. He spent the entire night watching his prisoner. To be on the safe side that no harm came to the prisoner from any mob violence, Chief Gurdane brought in several city employees to augment his small staff of police officers.

One of those city employees was L. R. Connor, who normally worked for the water department. He spent an extended period of time watching Edward. Edward told him about his travels since leaving Los Angeles. Edward asked if "extra" editions of newspapers had been put out with the story of his arrest. Edward began to cry when he spoke of his mother, saying, "There is no use bothering her. She hasn't enough money to do anything and may as well stay at home and try to bear it." Edward continued to deny killing Marion and repeated that "Andrew Cramer did it." At one time Edward lamented, "If I only had ditched the Hudson and grabbed a Ford in Seattle."

Los Angeles Chief of Police James Davis issued a statement to the media upon learning that Edward had been captured in Oregon:

> This is a triumph for American police methods and the American press. When they work in conjuncture they cannot be beaten. Cooperation of newspapers in broadcasting photographs and descriptions brought about the capture of Edward Hickman. It is another demonstration of the concentration of organized law forces against the criminal-he can't win.[7]

Upon learning that her son had been arrested, Edward's mother sent a telegram to the Umatilla County jail. The telegram read: "Be truthful and trust in God. I long to be with you. Cap Edwards said for me to wait. I am praying he will let me come." In response Edward sent a telegram that read:

> Dear Mother:
> I've received your word and also heard from father. I've confessed all I know. I kidnapped the girl but another killed her. This is the truth and I am ready to face what comes. Don't worry please for I'll stand the trial alone. Cap could recommend my past to authorities if he will.

Edward's father told reporters, "I couldn't believe he murdered the girl. I want to see him punished to the extent that he is guilty. I will be ready to help him all I can and I may be able to furnish him money to retain an attorney."

The committee in charge of the reward money decided to split the money between Chief Gurdane and Officer Lieuallen.

Shopkeeper George Willoughby who was the one to identify that Edward was in Seattle was disappointed in learning that he was that close to the wanted man and did not realize it in time to capture him and cash in on the reward money.

As the authorities in Pendleton waited for law enforcement from California to arrive, they spoke to Edward at length. He continued to blame Andrew Cramer for murdering Marion Parker. He expanded and said he met Andrew soon after he moved to Los Angeles from Kansas City. "It was on Thanksgiving Day that I met Cramer and a woman-I think her name was June Dunning. I had been living by holdups and thought it would be more profitable to work with an older man. Cramer was about 28 years old."

As Edward continued, he said that he and Cramer began to talk about kidnapping someone. As to how they settled on Marion, Edward said, "I had worked in the First National Bank of Los Angeles and knew how fond [Perry] Parker was of Marion."

Edward told of going to Marion's school and telling the teacher Perry was injured and taking Marion away. He recalled:

> She was a good little kid. I liked her and she didn't want to go with Cramer, but wished to stay with me. But we had to carry out our plan, which was for Cramer to hide the girl and for me to collect the money which I wanted to use in going through college. Cramer was more interested in the idea of kidnapping a child than in getting money. He only wanted $200 or $300 of the $1500 which we asked for in letters signed "The Fox" which I wrote.[8]

Edward said the next morning Cramer showed up at his apartment with a suitcase. He said he asked Cramer, "Where is the girl?" It was at that time, according to Edward, that Cramer opened the suitcase displaying the dismembered body of the child. Edward recalled: "I screamed and asked why he had 'gone ahead.'" To which Cramer replied, "She started crying and I had to stop her. As long as he had 'gone ahead' we decided to do what we could to get the money anyway. I thought Parker would be glad to get his daughter back regardless of her condition."

Edward told of seeing Marion, saying: "She looked rather natural. Cramer had put on her dress and her eyes were sewed to her eyebrows and she looked all right at first glance. She had been cut through the middle. I don't know what became of the other pieces, which Cramer did not give me. I guess he threw them away where police say they were found."[9]

Edward admitted stealing the automobile saying, "I stole the Hudson and drove to San Francisco. Cramer wasn't there, so I headed north because Southern California was so wrought up." Edward described driving to Seattle and back to Portland before heading towards Pendleton. As the interview wrapped up, Edward said, "I treated her as I would my own sister. I loved her and still do."

Los Angeles County District Attorney Keyes and Chief of Detectives Cline arrived in Pendleton to retrieve their prisoner. Edward was surrounded by heavily armed police officers and whisked away on a waiting train.

During the long train ride to Los Angeles, Edward reiterated the same story, blaming Cramer for the actual murder. At one point Edward asked for a pen and paper so he could write a letter to his mother. At this point, District Attorney Keyes told Edward: "Think of your mother and clear your conscience by telling the truth." Edward paused and then replied, "All right, I'll talk now, if you'll let me eat first." Some of the police officers who were standing guard hurriedly got some food for Edward who quickly devoured the meal.

Edward wrote out a full confession, this time taking full blame for the kidnapping and murder of Marion. Edward wrote that his first attempt to meet with Perry was cancelled after he spotted two police cars following Perry's car. He wrote that Marion was with him in his car and upon seeing her father's car, "Marion cried and wanted to go to her father. But I shut her up and drove away before they could spot me."

Once in Los Angeles, Edward was quickly taken by automobile to the jail by back roads and alleyways. The street where the jail was located was roped off so only the car carrying Edward could enter the street. Law enforcement feared mob violence. The streets surrounding the jail were overflowing with people hoping to catch a glimpse of Edward. Edward was booked into the county jail and assigned number 88783.

When Eva was informed that her son had confessed to murdering Marion, she broke down sobbing, still declaring that her son was innocent. Eva wrote a letter to Edward that read:

Dear Edward:
I want you to know that in spite of my grief and heartaches and the trouble you are in now, I still have faith in you and want you to be brave.

I, your brothers and sisters are still interested in your future and we are most anxious to see you through this and to know that you have not done what they think you have.

My son, you must have courage and fight. You must be the man you are, and trust and aid those who are there to defend you. In our present sorrow and unhappy experience it seems that the whole world is covered by dark clouds, but you can see, Edward, there must be a bright spot, for all clouds have a silver lining.

Edward, you are my son, my own flesh and blood, and no matter what has happened or ever will, I shall never lose my faith and love for you and shall be for you and with you to the very last. Your loving mother.[10]

A previous cellmate of Edward's, Werby Hunt, came forward with information implicating Edward in a robbery of a pharmacy the previous year. During the robbery, the owner of the pharmacy, Ivy Toms, was murdered and officer D. J. Oliver with the Los Angeles Police Department was shot but survived.

At the jail, Sheriff William Traeger feared for Edward's safety from the other inmates. He supplied the jail staff with a hundred rounds of tear gas should a problem arise. The potential violence towards Edward was not confined to the jail; the public was becoming increasingly enraged about the crime.

A crowd estimated to be in excess of 5,000 people arrived at the courthouse on the day of Edward's arraignment. Judge Carlos Hardy presided over the proceedings. Edward's mother hired attorney Jerome Walsh from Kansas City. The court granted him privileges to practice law in California. He asked for additional time to speak with his client and the court granted a postponement. Once the arraignment was held, Edward pled not guilty by reason of insanity.

Several interviews were conducted by professionals, all of whom deemed Edward to be sane. The prosecution spoke to numerous people in Kansas City who knew Edward. None of the interviews led the prosecution to believe that Edward had ever demonstrated any signs of insanity. Defense attorney Walsh's request for a postponement of the trial was denied. The next motion filed by the defense was to remove Judge Hardy from the trial citing his perceived prejudice against the case. Judge Hardy recused himself from the trial and Judge J. J. Trabucco was appointed.

The trial got underway with a jury consisting of eight men and four women. The defense claimed that Edward's confession was a sign of his insanity. The prosecution called numerous law enforcement officers to the stand. When the jury was shown photographs of Marion's dismembered body, several jurors became so distraught that Judge Trabucco called for an extended break. When the trial resumed, Detective Lieutenant Richard Lucas took the stand and explained that the details given by Edward in his confession could only have been done by a sane person. Chief of Detectives Cline told the jury that Edward acted completely sane while traveling from Pendleton to Los Angeles.

The prosecution called Dr. Thomas Orbison to the witness stand. He told the jury that after examining Edward, he found him to be not only sane, but also highly intelligent. He read a statement Edward wrote while in the Los Angeles jail:

Do the American people recognize crime?
  Have prisons helped to stop crime?
  Is one life worth the sacrifice that crime may be called to the attention of the people?
  Do the American people think they are safely protected from crime?
  Will the American people listen to me?

Will this jury listen to me?

Crime is threatening society, government welfare and the very destiny of the American people.

Crime was generated in me.

I am youth in crime.

If you hang me by the neck until dead or put me in a prison to rot with the Loebs and Leopolds, will this help to stop criminal tendencies?

Some people will be gratified, others disappointed, but will it solve crime?

Loeb and Leopold were sentenced to life, Mrs. Snyder and Gray to death, and Remus to the asylum, but how has this stopped crime?

If you kill me how will that stop crime?

I am beginning this pleading with you not from a selfish standpoint to save my own life. It is for your own welfare that I make this plea that my crime be made to do some good.

I don't fear death; I don't care what happens to me. Providence guided me in this act that the American people might be given a terrible warning of the trend of crime.[11]

By the end of the trial, eight witnesses testified that Edward was sane; while three witnesses claimed he was insane.

Marion's father took the witness stand and told of finding his daughter's body moments after handing over $1,500 in ransom money.

Edward's father told the court it would be unjust to hang Edward as he was not responsible for his actions: "Edward is crazy, as crazy as he can be. It would be wrong if California took the life of a crazy boy. He should be put in an asylum for the rest of his life, for I realize how dangerous he is. Any madman is dangerous."

"I loathe the ground he walks upon," exclaimed District Attorney Keyes in his closing arguments. He told the jury he was speaking "for the rights of not only the people of California, but for the rights of the people of the entire United States."

District Attorney Keyes went onto say: "It was only for the fact that we are civilized that a mob did not take this man from the officers of the law, and if it was not that I was an officer of the law, I should have wanted to be in the front ranks of such a mob to help put a rope around this man's neck."

District Attorney Keyes stressed his belief that Edward was completely sane: "From the day of his arrest, when he threw a fit in [the]Pendleton jail, the Fox knew he was trapped, and he has played his insanity dodge to fool the police, fool the district attorney, fool his attorneys, and you, the jury, because he knew it was the only chance to escape the punishment of the law."[12]

Judge Trabucco gave the jury their final instructions by saying, "You are instructed that the sole issue for you to decide is the issue of whether or not the defendant was sane or insane at the time of the crime."

The courtroom was filled to capacity with people standing in the back and even standing on chairs to get a better view when the buzzer rang, indicating the jury had reached a verdict. Edward's mother, father, and siblings were in the courtroom when the jury filed in with the verdict. A hush fell over the courtroom as the verdict was read. The jury found Edward to be sane.

Edward's mother collapsed upon hearing the verdict. Edward told the reporters:

I know I'm sane. If I had all the things the matter with me that the experts said I had, it would be as bad as hanging. I know I'll hang. What about it? I haven't anything more to live for. But I hope they don't make it too soon. Not that I care for myself, but it seems a pity to waste the opportunity to study me. Perhaps the scientists could find out something to help them discover and control youthful criminals.[13]

Days after the trial, Judge Trabucco formally sentenced Edward to be hanged at San Quentin prison on April 27, 1928. Edward's attorneys immediately filed an appeal.

While waiting on the appeal, Edward was formally tried for the murder of Ivy Toms, the pharmacist who was killed during a robbery that Edward and Welby Hunt committed in December 1926. Edward and Welby were convicted and sentenced to life in prison.

The appeal was denied, and the execution date loomed. Edward's father made a plea to the warden with an affidavit from a psychiatrist who examined Edward prior to the trial and declared him to be insane. The warden opted to not pursue additional sanity examinations. Edward's father took his plea to California Governor Young.

Thomas told reporters: "I am going to ask Governor Young to believe my son insane and give him a life sentence. Failing in this, I will go to San Quentin Thursday and say good-by [sic] to him. That's all I'm here for. I want to see Edward again before he pays for his crime." Governor Young declined to intervene, as did the United States Supreme Court.

In the days leading up to the execution, Edward confessed to several other crimes. He sent a letter to Dallas, Texas, Chief of Police Claude Trammel. In the letter, Edward confessed to robbing a grocery store and a pharmacy in Dallas in 1926. The detectives who worked on the case believed the description of the robbery suspect matched Edward.

In another letter, Edward asked the Muskogee, Oklahoma, chief of police and the citizens of Muskogee to forgive him for robbing a restaurant in December 1926. Edward explained he wanted to repay the restaurant owner, but he lacked the funds to do so.

The next letter Edward wrote was to the chief of detectives in Columbus, Ohio. Edward confessed in the letter to having robbed four establishments in

Columbus in 1927. He stated in the letter that he was "heartily sorry for having done wrong against the people of Columbus and hoped there would be no more crime in Columbus."

Chief of Police Jonathan Marshall received a letter from Edward confessing to driving a stolen vehicle and crashing into a light post in Ottawa, Kansas, in December 1926. When asked, Chief Marshall recalled the accident but did not suspect that Edward was responsible at the time.

The final letter written by Edward was to St. Louis, Missouri, Chief of Police Gerk. Edward confessed to holding up three drugstores in St. Louis in November 1927. He admitted to receiving $200 between all three robberies.

Edward was moved to a death cell at San Quentin prison. He visited with his father one last time. Edward's mother remained in Kansas, but she sent him one last letter, as did three other members of his family. Edward wrote a letter to his mother, his uncle, and defense attorney Walsh. He spent his final hours reading a bible and speaking with Reverend William Fleming who converted him to Catholicism.

Edward requested a phonograph and flowers for his death cell. He played a few records on the phonograph as the hours dragged on. He woke at 3 a.m. and asked the guard to play some jazz records. For Edward's final breakfast, he ate ham, eggs, cereal, fried potatoes, hot rolls, a waffle, milk, and coffee. Edward spoke to death watch guard Charles Aiston at length, describing his criminal career beginning at the age of twelve with a holdup.

The Parker family went into seclusion on the day of Edward's execution, as did Edward's mother in Kansas. Although Edward once said, "I wish they would arrange to hang me on a Friday the 13th," he was hanged on October 19, 1928, ten months after the murder of Marion. Edward was accompanied to the gallows by Reverend Fleming. As 200 spectators watched, Edward climbed the thirteen steps of the gallows and was hanged at 10:10 a.m.

4

Frank Egan and Dr. Nathan Housman

Earl Leter, age twenty-five, described for Detective Captain Dullea what happened on the night of June 10, 1931 when he was shot at a café owned by Harold McGuire:

> I know who did it and I'll take care of it of these guys myself. I'm not going to die. Don't bother me anymore. I'm not talking. I will say this: "McGuire had no more to do with it than you did. As to who did, I'll get him … I'll get well …" It happened during a fight—I was too drunk to know what caused the fight or to see who fired the shot. A man was standing over me, ready to kick me, when I recognized McGuire. He had come forward and, as well as I could hear him, was telling the man he'd better lay off me. Then someone shot. You know the rest.[1]

Before Earl could finish telling Captain Dullea what happened, he lapsed into unconsciousness and was rushed into emergency surgery to remove the bullet lodged in his abdomen. Ten minutes into the surgery, Earl was pronounced dead.

The police investigation revealed after the shooting that a friend of Earl's, Edward Chiasso, rushed him to a hotel room nearby. Edward then summoned a friend of theirs, Dr. Nathan Housman, to render aid. The police knew Earl and Edward were involved with the mafia, and it was a common practice among the underground figures to contact Dr. Housman when they did not want to attract the attention of medical staff.

Although there were approximately forty witnesses, no one was willing to talk to the police. The detectives questioned Edward about the sequence of events, but he simply said he found Earl lying in the street and believed he was ill. He said he took Earl back to his hotel room so he could rest. He then discovered Earl had been shot and summoned Dr. Housman, who rushed Earl to a hospital. The police released Edward after questioning him.

Despite Earl's statement that Harold was not responsible, the police issued an arrest warrant for him, charging him with murder. His attorney surrendered Harold, who posted $20,000 bail and was released from custody.

A grand jury was summoned, but the underground figures were reticent to testify. One witness testified: "I was too drunk to know much. Somebody stuck a gun in my back and told me to get 'em up. I did like I was told and they put me out." After testifying, the witness was approached in the hallway of the courthouse by gang leader Eddie Quinnones and told, "Dummy up." Another witness explained he was at the café but left before the shooting took place. Others refused to testify out of fear of incriminating themselves.

As one witness after another refused to offer a glimpse into how the shooting took place, Captain Dullea tried a different tactic. Figuring that Dr. Housman knew who the shooter was, he placed a hidden dictagraph machine in Dr. Housman's office. The investigators listened to every conversation that took place in Dr. Housman's office twenty-four hours a day.

A month later, the district attorney admitted they did not have a solid case and Judge George Schonfeld dismissed the case against Harold.

What the district attorney and the judge were not aware of is that the investigators uncovered another crime while listening to the conversations recorded on the dictagraph machine. They listened as City of San Francisco Public Defender Frank Egan and Dr. Housman discussed murdering a female, Mrs. Jessie Hughes. Nothing came of the investigation, and it was forgotten until a year later.

Several neighbors of the St. Francis Wood District in San Francisco noticed a large automobile circling their neighborhood multiple times during the night of April 29, 1932. The last time they saw the automobile, it was traveling at a high rate of speed with its headlights off. Soon after, a neighbor found a woman lying in the gutter who had been badly beaten. The police arrived and tried to determine the identity of the female.

At first, the police believed the woman had been a victim of a hit-and-run driver. However, they did not believe the hit and run had occurred where the body was located. Instead, they thought the crime occurred somewhere else and the female had been thrown from a moving car and landed in the gutter.

One of the woman's neighbors, John Kane, identified the victim as Mrs. Jessie Hughes, age fifty-seven. Her son, John, was killed by an automobile in 1918 when he was fourteen years old. She had been living alone ever since her husband died years before.

When the detectives arrived at Mrs. Hughes' house, they discovered all of the doors were locked and bolted from the inside, with the only access being from the garage. They knew Mrs. Hughes did not have a purse or any keys with her when she was found. They did not notice any signs of a robbery within the house. The detectives took photographs of the tire tracks on Mrs. Hughes' driveway.

The autopsy revealed Mrs. Hughes died from a crushed chest and liver. One side of her face was covered with friction burns. The coroner and the pathologist believed Mrs. Hughes was alive when she was run over by a car. However, they were not able to determine if she was conscious at the time. Mrs. Hughes was buried at the Holy Cross cemetery after a service at the Holstead Chapel in San Francisco.

Frank Egan came forward saying he had been a long-time friend of Mrs. Hughes. He told reporters she had almost been killed by an automobile a year before and had narrowly missed being hit by a car a week before. He explained she enjoyed going for walks in the evening, despite his warnings of the danger. Frank gave the reporters some statistics regarding how many people had been killed or injured by automobiles in the San Francisco Bay Area during the previous year.

The police sent out teletypes statewide looking for the automobile described by the witnesses. However, they were not completely convinced an automobile was the cause of Mrs. Hughes death; they were also considering the possibility she had been murdered. The police clarified: "It is possible that Mrs. Hughes was the victim of robbers, who beat her to death and then ran over her in their automobile to make it appear as if she had been struck by a machine."

As the investigation got underway, the police interviewed Mrs. Hughes' neighbors. One neighbor recalled seeing an automobile back out of the Hughes' garage. Another neighbor told the investigators she observed a car in front of Mrs. Hughes' house days before the crime. A friend of Mrs. Hughes told the detectives she spoke to Mrs. Hughes four hours before she was found on the roadway. She recalled Mrs. Hughes hearing the doorbell in her house and saying, "It might be someone trying to get me."

The detectives learned that Frank was the principal beneficiary in Mrs. Hughes' will and her insurance policies. The investigators learned that Frank had purchased life insurance policies for Mrs. Hughes and paid the premiums. The insurance agent told the investigators that he originally turned down the request that Mrs. Hughes have a $10,000 policy and instead offered a $5,000 policy, which he felt was sufficient. The insurance agent recalled Frank insisting that the policy be for $10,000 and that he be the beneficiary. The insurance agent told the investigators that when Frank had financial difficulties, he cancelled one of his own policies in order to continue paying the policy on Mrs. Hughes.

While the detectives were running down leads, they received an anonymous letter stating Frank had made a previous attempt on Mrs. Hughes' life. The writer of the letter claimed Frank had attempted to poison Mrs. Hughes, causing her to be hospitalized until she regained her strength.

Witnesses came forward saying Frank and Dr. Housman were seen together the night Mrs. Hughes was murdered. They were seen at a local bar and were heard arguing and throwing things at one another. The police believed this was done as a ruse to provide an alibi for the evening.

Detectives interviewed Frank about his involvement with the death of Mrs. Hughes, but all he would say was he had been friends with Mrs. Hughes for many years. He told the detectives he met Mrs. Hughes after the San Francisco earthquake and fire in 1906 when he saw her on the street with her son. She was dragging a trunk and a sewing machine, her only possessions after the fire. Frank explained he was driving a Wells Fargo wagon and stopped to help them. He took Mrs. Hughes and her son to his sister's house where they were able to stay for an extended period of time. Frank said she referred to him as her "son."

The investigation into the murder of Mrs. Hughes led the police to an associate of Frank's, Albert Tinnin. Albert was convicted of attempting to murder Marjorie Crockett in 1918. Marjorie and her sister, Helen Kincaid, inherited a large estate from their mother. Albert was living with Helen in San Francisco at the time. Helen hired Frank to represent her in contesting the will. At the time, Frank was an attorney in private practice in San Francisco. Helen believed her mother was not of sound mind when she gave a larger portion of her estate to Marjorie.

Albert knew if Marjorie were to die, Helen would inherit the entire estate. Albert allegedly took a train to Corning, California, where Marjorie and her husband John lived. He checked into a hotel using an alias. Albert went to Marjorie's house when she was home alone. Albert told Marjorie he was an attorney representing Helen who had filed a lawsuit regarding her share of the inheritance. Marjorie allowed him into the house but became suspicious and headed to her telephone to call her husband. Before Marjorie could reach the telephone, Albert grabbed her and placed a cloth with chloroform over her mouth. Marjorie sank to the floor and Albert ran out the door. In his hurried state, he did not latch the door and the wind blew the door open, bringing a breeze into the house. Marjorie did not succumb to the chloroform because of the breeze blowing through the house. She came to and contacted her husband and the local sheriff's office.

The Tehama Sheriff's Department immediately began searching for Albert. They notified all law enforcement in the surrounding areas. Tehama County Sheriff Clifford Moller asked the San Francisco Police Department to try and locate Albert, but they were unable to find him. Albert had seemingly vanished. Two years later, the police received information that Albert was at Frank's office in San Francisco. The police arrested him and delivered him to the Tehama County jail.

A trial was held in Tehama County, and Albert was convicted of attempted murder despite Frank providing him with an alibi. Albert managed to escape from the Tehama County jail but was soon located and sent to San Quentin prison. Frank was instrumental in getting an early release for Albert after he served nine years at San Quentin prison. Albert had only been free a short time before Mrs. Hughes was murdered.

The police also wanted to talk to another associate of Frank's, Verne Doran, age twenty-three, regarding Mrs. Hughes' murder. A year before Mrs. Hughes was killed, Frank managed to get Verne released early from prison where he was serving time for a burglary charge. After being released from prison, Verne became Frank's chauffeur.

The police wanted to question Albert and Verne regarding the death of Mrs. Hughes. While they were searching for the two men, Frank phoned Captain Dullea and stated: "They've got me, two men have got me here. I'm in a booth in the Ferry Building. They think I'm phoning home. I'm innocent Captain." Just as Captain Dullea started to ask Frank who he was with, the phone call was disconnected. Police officers rushed to the Ferry Building, but no one was there.

Frank and his wife, Lorraine, lived in San Francisco with their three young sons. Their house had gone into foreclosure two months before Mrs. Hughes was murdered. Detectives interviewed Frank's wife, Lorraine, after they received the phone call. All she could tell them was Frank said he had to attend a Native Sons' dinner and would be home late. Lorraine told the investigators she received a telephone call from a man who simply said, "We have taken Frank for a ride." Lorraine received the phone call minutes after Frank called Captain Dullea.

The investigators learned Frank did not attend the dinner he told his wife about. They learned he met with Dr. Housman at the Phelan building where Dr. Housman had an office. Frank then went to his own office where he met with an unidentified man, according to the elevator operator at Frank's building.

The investigators also learned hours before Frank called Captain Dullea, he voiced his frustration to a friend, private investigator William Otts, telling him that the police were spying on him. Frank also complained to William that the police were tapping his business telephone line, listening in on all of his conversations.

While the police were searching for Frank after he phoned Captain Dullea, they located his car in a parking garage close to his office. They noticed a "few dents and scratches on the right fender."

The grand jury met for an emergency session while Frank was still missing. An order was granted for the police to search Frank's office as well as his home. The state of California assigned their own investigators to assist with the case.

Theodore Roche, president of the police commission admitted to reporters they had, "a large amount of confidential information." They believed they would locate Frank in the San Francisco Bay Area and therefore they did not send any teletypes to other law enforcement agencies in California.

Captain Dullea told reporters:

> We want an explanation of the entire affair. We don't understand Egan's disappearance or the telephone messages. We do not believe he was at the Ferry Building when the call was made. In fact we have reports from two sources that he was on Powell Street at about the same time as he called me. Egan is a city official and everything possible is being done to find him and clear up this mystery.[2]

The police assigned twenty-two detectives to locate Frank.

Days later, Frank's attorney, Vincent Hallinan, told reporters that Frank was willing to surrender. He explained that Frank was in a sanitarium and would not be speaking to the authorities on the advice of his doctor. He confirmed that Frank had not been held captive by anyone and entered the sanitarium on his own free will. Frank's attorney issued the following statement:

> It is nobody's business. I am Egan's attorney and have instructed him not to say anything. He will not talk to the police. He does not feel obliged to explain the telephone call to Captain Dullea. Further, he is not going to be badgered about this thing. His name has been linked with the death of a woman and innuendos have been made. The whole thing is ridiculous.
>
> Frank J. Egan has not been in hiding nor has he made any effort to conceal his whereabouts or identity. He feels he is entitled to the ordinary privilege of a citizen to be protected in his private and personnel affairs from inquiries or annoyance.
>
> Shortly after the death of Mrs. Hughes Egan was in communication with the police and ready and willing to furnish them with any information in his possession. They assured him they were convinced the death was the cause of a hit-and-run accident and he accepted their version.
>
> Meanwhile a detail of the homicide squad visited his home, measured his tires, questioned his domestics and otherwise showed active and aggressive suspicion, as implied by questions on his whereabouts the night of Mrs. Hughes' death, that he had been concerned in it.
>
> They afterwards discovered that for some two hours or more prior to the finding of the unfortunate woman's body that Egan had been attending prizefights where he was seen by numerous disinterested persons, and his automobile had been parked in a public garage.
>
> Nevertheless and apparently upon the sole consideration that he was reputed to be her beneficiary under her will, Egan and his family and his private affairs have been subjected to harassing, annoying and unwarranted scrutiny. It is now reported the police department desires to question him further with regard to other alleged aspects of the matter.
>
> With Mrs. Hughes' death Egan has not the remotest connection. Nevertheless he will apparently be subjected to further annoyance. He is not accused of any crime, no indictment or warrant has been issued or demanded and he will no longer allow this matter to be made the basis of an inquiry into his personal matters in no way connected with this.[3]

Days later, the police announced they had located the vehicle believed to have been used to kill Mrs. Hughes. They believed the tires matched the tire tracks of those in her garage. The vehicle did not belong to either Albert or Verne, but instead had been loaned to Verne for the day. The owner of the car was a friend of Frank's, Oscar Postel.

The police arrested four individuals with connections to Albert and Verne. The men led the detectives to Albert. Captain Dullea arrested Albert at a hotel in San Francisco. He initially provided a false name to Captain Dullea before admitting his true identity. Albert had a firearm in his possession when he was arrested, which added a charge of being a felon in possession of a firearm.

Albert claimed to have been with a friend, Mrs. Barton, when Mrs. Hughes was killed. Years before, Frank represented Mrs. Barton when she was charged with oil swindling, but she was acquitted. Days after Albert provided an alibi, he had a change of heart and said: "Maybe I shouldn't have mentioned that. But I guess it's too late to take back that alibi now."

Verne's mother hired an attorney who told the police Verne was "in hiding." After almost three weeks in hiding, Verne's attorney made arrangements for him to surrender to the police. He did surrender, but he refused to answer any questions put forth by the detectives. Once he was in custody, the police charged him with a new case of robbery. The robbery occurred three months prior to the murder. The victim identified Verne and another man as the ones responsible for robbing him. Verne was transferred to San Quentin prison for a parole violation from his prior burglary charge while he waited for the trial to begin for the murder of Mrs. Hughes.

Soon after, Coroner Leland announced that Frank, Albert, and Verne would be required to answer questions at the coroner's inquest. Frank remained in the sanitarium and claimed he was suffering from amnesia. He refused to accept the subpoena to testify at the coroner's inquest until San Francisco Mayor Rossi threatened to remove him as the city's public defender for misconduct. As the public learned more about the case, they became very vocal about wanting Frank removed from office. Frank claimed the police were trying to "get him" due to an ongoing feud. Frank's attorney told reporters that Frank was being made to be the "goat."

At the coroner's inquest, Frank refused to answer any questions on the grounds that his testimony "might tend to establish a crime with which he might be charged" according to his attorney. He also refused to turn over any financial documents pertaining to Mrs. Hughes. During the coroner's inquest, Frank became agitated when other evidence was presented. He interrupted the proceedings, shouting that the police were lying. Formal charges of misconduct were filed against Frank, and he was suspended from his job as a public defender for the city of San Francisco.

Faced with having to answer questions at the coroner's inquest, Verne decided to confess at his mother's urging. His mother met with San Francisco Chief of Police William Quinn, District Attorney Matthew Brady, Assistant District Attorney Isidore Golden, and Captain Dullea in an effort to procure a reduced sentence for her son. She explained to the authorities that "Egan has been a bad influence." Verne's attorney arranged for him to turn state's evidence in exchange for a shorter prison sentence. With all sides agreeing to the reduced sentence, Verne agreed to tell everything he knew about the murder.

Verne began by explaining to the detectives that he felt a tremendous obligation to Frank because he had arranged for him to be released early from prison. Verne went onto explain that he and Albert murdered Mrs. Hughes at the request of Frank, who stood to gain financially.

Verne described in detail the events surrounding the murder of Mrs. Hughes. He said Frank began complaining about Mrs. Hughes "pestering" him about money he owed her. He expanded by saying she had filed a complaint with the California Bar Association and was making his life "miserable." According to Verne, Frank told him it was either his life or her life and he had a plan to get rid of her. Verne said when he resisted being involved, Frank reminded him he would be in prison, were it not for him.

Verne said Frank introduced him to Albert and the three of them had meetings in the days leading up to the murder. Verne recalled the three of them drove out to Half Moon Bay and Albert practiced shooting a pistol. The final meeting, Verne said, was held at Albert's hotel room at the Blackstone Hotel in San Francisco.

On the morning of the murder, Verne said he borrowed Oscar's car, telling him that Frank wanted to borrow the car. In as much as Verne was Frank's chauffeur, Oscar agreed to the request. Verne said later that morning Frank and Albert stopped by his house. He said Frank gave Albert $5 and instructed him to go to Mrs. Hughes' house and pay her the money. The reason for this, Verne explained, was for Albert to become familiar with the house.

According to Verne, the final meeting was held that evening in Frank's office. It was agreed that when Verne and Albert were within five minutes of Mrs. Hughes' house, they would use a pay phone and call Frank at his office. He, in turn, would call Mrs. Hughes and tell her he would be at her house within five minutes. That way, Verne explained, Mrs. Hughes would open the garage door so he could drive directly into the garage, as was his custom when he visited her.

Verne said the plan worked perfectly and Mrs. Hughes met them in the garage. When she realized Frank was not with them, they assured her he had gotten out of the car a block before when he saw someone he knew at the theater. Verne said they encouraged her to put her coat and hat on and walk down to the theater and find Frank. Verne explained to the detectives they wanted Mrs. Hughes to be in her coat and hat when she was found, so it would appear she had been struck by a car while out walking. Verne explained that Frank had told them it was common practice for Mrs. Hughes to go for a walk in the evening.

Verne went into details as to how the murder took place. He said when Mrs. Hughes refused to put her coat and hat on, Albert struck her with brass knuckles, rendering her unconscious. Albert then yelled for Verne to start the car while he placed Mrs. Hughes' body directly in front of the front tire. Albert told Verne to drive back and forth over the body, which Verne admitted to doing. Verne said they placed Mrs. Hughes in the trunk of the car and Verne backed the car out of the garage while Albert closed the garage door. Once the garage door was closed, Verne said Albert got into the trunk of the car with the body. Verne said they drove a short while until he found a spot out of view, and Albert tossed the body out of the trunk onto the street.

He explained after the murder, they left Oscar's vehicle in his garage, and they proceeded back to Albert's hotel room where they met with Frank. Verne said Frank spent the evening at a bar in order to have an alibi. He expanded by saying, once Frank arrived at the hotel room, he immediately asked how things went with Mrs. Hughes. Verne said he and Albert assured Frank the job had been completed, but they both expressed regret for having been involved. Verne said the three of them drove around in Frank's car until 2 a.m. before Frank dropped them off and insisted that they leave town.

Once Verne finished his confession, San Francisco Police Chief Quinn prepared arrest warrants for Frank and Albert. They located Albert and arrested him on a charge of first-degree murder. Frank, however, had once again disappeared. A team of police officers and detectives went to Frank's house with the warrant for his arrest. Lorraine said Frank was not at home and she did not know his whereabouts.

A California Highway Patrol officer recalled seeing Frank driving in San Mateo County before it was announced he was wanted for murder. The San Francisco Police Department sent a teletype to all police agencies notifying them of the arrest warrant for Frank. The teletype read:

All Points Bulletin from: San Fran Control No 2
Emergency
06/04/1932 8:04 p.m.
Wanted for Murder!!!
Arrest and hold for murder one Frank J. Egan, described as follows:
50 yrs., about 5 feet 11 inches, weight about 155 lbs., (very thin).

Sallow complexion, face very thin and sunken, exposing cheek bones, black hair, graying, bald in front with tuft of curly black hair standing straight up. Last seen at Tanforan, in San Mateo County, between 2:15 and 2:30 pm this date, driving south in a blue Lincoln sedan, California state license No. 6-E-4. If arrested, notify this department and an officer will be sent for him immediately. Wm J Quinn, Chief of Police, San Francisco, (JMF) NM Release.[4]

Dr. Housman told the authorities he was willing to tell them everything he knew. He agreed he had been friends with Frank for years. He admitted he had signed prescriptions for Mrs. Hughes and had treated her from time to time. He also admitted to meeting Verne through Frank. He denied that Verne and Frank ever asked him what injuries a hit-and-run victim would have. He continually agreed to cooperate saying, "I'll tell all I know at any time."

After three days on the lam, Frank suddenly appeared at the Golden Gate Park Police Station in San Francisco. Defense attorney Hallinan stressed to the media: "Frank is innocent and he never avoided arrest. He was not trying to escape. His first intimation of any grand jury action reached him at 3 a.m. today. Frank has been made the victim of a plot. At the proper time we will go into court and prove Egan's absolute innocence."

The man who spent his entire career trying to keep his clients out of jail was booked into the San Francisco County jail as prisoner 154. Frank refused to have his fingerprints or photograph taken, although he did allow newspaper reporters to take his photograph.

Frank, his attorney, and Chief of Police Quinn held a joint press conference. Frank told Chief Quinn, "I know you to be honest and conscientious." Defense attorney Hallinan told reporters:

> The police made it tough for me to surrender Egan. I had arranged for him to come in at 10 a.m. today, but they put police in my house last night and kept them there. I would have been unable to act, so I got in touch with Frank and told him to go on in.
>
> I am convinced the police will do all in their power to prevent Frank Egan from ever securing a fair trial. I read with amazement their shameful compromise with an acknowledged red-handed murderer and their agreement to grant immunity to him for supplying his lying testimony, the only evidence that will enable them to construct a case against Frank Egan.[5]

Verne, accompanied by four homicide detectives, returned to the crime scene so he could walk them through every detail of what happened.

Meanwhile, Albert's attorney assured the media Albert had a "perfect alibi" for the night Mrs. Hughes was killed. However, Chief Quinn told reporters: "Tinnin has maintained the same silence regarding this crime that Doran and Frank J. Egan did up to the time of Doran's confession. I have heard no statements Tinnin has made that would tend to clear him. He is tied to the crime by Doran's confession just as tightly as Doran is."

At Frank's arraignment, he refused to answer any questions and was held in contempt of court. At his next court appearance, he pled not guilty. Due to Frank's ongoing legal case, the San Francisco City Council voted to dismiss Frank as the city's public defender.

Armed with the knowledge that Frank was involved with the murder of Mrs. Hughes, the police took another look at some other cases.

Four years before, Margaret Busch, age sixty-five, died at her home in San Francisco. Her relatives in Chicago filed a lawsuit claiming Frank and his wife,

Lorraine, took advantage of Margaret's declining mental capabilities. They claimed that Lorraine's aunt, Maud Wilson, took advantage of Margaret by claiming to be a spiritualist who was able to communicate directly with Jesus Christ, Moses, angels, and Margaret's relatives who had previously died. Margaret's relatives alleged Frank, Lorraine, and Maud convinced Margaret to leave her $240,000 estate to the Egans.

Frank issued a statement to the press denying any wrongdoing: "If the Chicago relatives, who are merely second cousins, held such a warm place in the affection of Miss Busch why did they not visit her within the eleven years before her death?" The lawsuit was settled out of court.

The police also revisited the death of Mrs. Hughes' brother, James. He was found dead on the railroad tracks in San Francisco. The coroner believed James had been shot to death and then placed on the railroad tracks to make it look like an accident. Frank appeared as a witness at the coroner's inquest. Nothing could be proven, and the case was closed as an accident. After examining the case again, the authorities could not prove anything beyond an accident.

Edward Cook asked the court to exhume his wife's body. He explained after learning about the Hughes case, he became concerned Frank and Dr. Housman may have poisoned his wife, Florence, who died three months before Mrs. Hughes. He explained Dr. Housman had been her doctor and Frank had business dealings with her. He claimed there was $5,000 that Frank never accounted for. The body was exhumed but there was no sign of any poison.

A woman by the name of Mrs. Emerson came forward with information about Frank. She explained that Frank represented her when he was in private practice after she caused an automobile accident. Frank, she said, demanded that she sign over her house to him so the opposing party could not take the house in judgment. He also wanted $8,000 in fees after he won the case in court. Detectives later learned Frank gave Mrs. Emerson's house to Oscar, the registered owner of the car that the police believed was the one used to kill Mrs. Hughes.

The investigators learned that Frank was threatened with a lawsuit two days before Mrs. Hughes was murdered. The crux of the lawsuit was Frank's failure to repay $8,120 to August and Katie Weber. August allegedly loaned Frank $5,000 after Frank obtained a job for August working for the city in the street department. That loan was never repaid before August died in 1930. At that time, his wife, Katie, was owed money from August's pension fund. The lawsuit claimed that Frank took the entire $3,120 from the pension fund and placed it in Katie's bank account but promptly withdrew it without her knowledge. Prior to Katie's death, she hired an attorney to attempt to collect the debt. The attorney told reporters: "Two days before Egan disappeared, I made a final demand for the balance and told him that unless it was forthcoming at once I intended to take drastic measures to recover it." Katie's relatives turned over a letter they received from her days before she died. In the letter Katie wrote:

The lawyer whom you met at August's funeral—his best friend—we entrusted everything to him. He did that. He forged the names. I can't describe it at all. What a rotten dog he is! Now I am going to tell you something that happened to me. I wanted to draw something from the bank. There was only $4 out of $8,125. You can imagine how I felt. I can't eat and I can't sleep. I am so emaciated you could look right through me. I feel as though I should like to die. Only $4 to my name.[6]

Four months after Mrs. Hughes was murdered, a combined trial for Frank and Albert got underway. Superior Court Judge Frank Dunne was appointed to preside over the case. The state of California was represented by Prosecutor Idador Golden. Frank was represented by defense attorney Vincent Hallinan and Albert was represented by Nathan Coghlan. After eighty people were summoned for jury duty, six men and six women were selected to serve on the jury. The courtroom was filled to overflowing every day of the trial. Of the 108 seats in the courtroom, one was occupied by Frank's wife, and one by Verne's mother.

The jury heard that Frank allegedly advised Mrs. Hughes to deed her house to a friend of his. The friend, Richard Kazaka, borrowed $1,750 against the house through a bank. He gave Frank $500 and kept the rest of the money. Mrs. Hughes never received any money from the transaction and the house ended up in foreclosure. Richard arranged for a sale of the property, and Frank received the proceeds from the sale of the house. Richard took the witness stand and admitted Mrs. Hughes did not receive any money from the sale of her house. The vice president of the bank, a representative of the title company, and the new owners of the property all testified that Mrs. Hughes never received any compensation for her house.

The prosecution explained to the jury that Frank owed more than $17,000 at the time Mrs. Hughes was killed. Frank, the prosecution alleged, encouraged Mrs. Hughes to take out two life insurance policies. The policies were non-contestable and were to pay twice the amount if the death was deemed an accident. The prosecution explained that Frank paid the premiums for Mrs. Hughes, while letting his own life insurance policies lapse.

The attorney representing the bank where the Egans had their mortgage testified that the Egan's personal residence was in foreclosure. He told the jury Frank asked that his wife not be notified because he had spent the money that she gave him for the mortgage on other things.

You could hear a pin drop in the courtroom as Verne made his way to the witness stand. He kept his eyes cast downward and spoke in a quiet voice. The prosecution asked Verne to describe what happened between Frank and Mrs. Hughes. Verne quietly stated: "He said Mrs. Hughes was hounding him so much that he dared go to his office only at noon. We first discussed killing her while we were in Egan's automobile, parked in front of a church, Egan said it was quiet there."

Verne explained how they borrowed Oscar's car and then drove to Mrs. Hughes' house. He confirmed that Frank then phoned Mrs. Hughes when they were on their way to her house and asked her to open the garage door for them. Verne confirmed Albert hit Mrs. Hughes prior to placing her on the floor of the garage. In a barely audible voice, Verne confirmed he drove the car over Mrs. Hughes' body before placing her in the trunk of the automobile. Verne confirmed he drove a short distance while looking for a quiet place to leave the body. Albert, he said, tossed the body where it was located.

Verne told the jury he and Albert returned the car to Oscar before meeting with Frank. When asked if he and Albert received any compensation for the murder, Verne simply said Frank bought them new hats the day after the murder.

Oscar testified about receiving a frantic phone call from a male demanding, "Get rid of that car quick." Oscar told the court that he explained to the caller, "It's too late, the cops have taken it away."

A friend of Frank's, Oliver Wissell, took the witness stand and admitted Frank had previously spoken of having financial problems. Prosecutor Golden asked, "Didn't Egan tell you there was no way of his getting his money from Mrs. Hughes unless she died?" Oliver reluctantly admitted Frank had said those words. Oliver also admitted Frank had arranged for the government to return his boat after he had been caught with liquor during Prohibition on four separate occasions.

Lieutenant Francis Latulippe, head of the San Francisco Police Department's Ballistics Bureau, presented large photographs of the evidence he studied while investigating the murder: "This is the tire tread on the garage floor. This, the tread of the front wheel of the borrowed car. The photographs are of the same tread." He also told the jury the gray hairs in the trunk of the car compared to Mrs. Hughes' hair.

Albert, who referred to himself as a "graduate of Folsom" (prison) took the witness stand. He clearly laid out every detail of his activities on the night Mrs. Hughes was murdered as well as the day before. However, he was not able to recall any of his activities on the afternoon of the murder, when the prosecution alleged that he and Verne met with Frank.

Albert testified he was at a hotel that he could not remember the name of, nor could he remember the name of the woman he was with. He claimed he spent the evening of the murder with his alibi, Mrs. Barton.

Prosecutor Golden asked Albert how he met Frank. Albert explained he first met Frank when he was incarcerated. The prosecution went through Albert's criminal history pointing out that Frank was his attorney each time he was in trouble with the law.

The prosecution asked several questions about Albert's conviction for the attempted murder of Marjorie Crockett. It was pointed out to the jury that Frank provided Albert with an alibi for the time frame that Marjorie was attacked. During cross examination, Albert admitted Frank was responsible for his early release from prison when he was serving time for the attempted murder of Marjorie. Albert also admitted he worked for Frank as a process server when needed.

When a group of reporters asked Frank's defense attorney if Frank planned to take the witness stand, he angrily replied: "Frank Egan is his own boss. If he determines to take the stand I can't stop him, of course. But I have advised him not to testify, and I am quite positive that he will heed my advice. If he does not, he can look for another attorney." Frank said he was eager to tell "everything at the proper time and place."[7]

The proper time and place came to be in the courtroom despite the advice of Frank's defense attorney. Frank's testimony did not get off to a good start, with numerous arguments between Frank and the prosecution. After Judge Dunne threatened to remove Frank from the witness stand, Albert's defense attorney encouraged Frank to answer the questions put forth by the prosecution.

Frank, who was used to asking the questions in the courtroom, found himself on the opposite side. Frank evaded all questions about his financial involvement with Mrs. Hughes, the night she was murdered, and his disappearances. By the time he stepped down from the witness stand, the jury knew no more than they had before he was sworn in.

During closing arguments, defense attorney Hallinan interrupted prosecutor Golden a number of times until Judge Dunne said: "Mr. Hallinan, your conduct is noisy, offensive, obstreperous and contemptuous. I find you in contempt, and as punishment I sentence you to be confined in the county jail for a period of twenty-four hours—I assign Mr. Coghlan to represent the defendant Egan."

Defense attorney Hallinan responded, "I want to take an exception to the order being entered at this time and in the presence of the jury. I ask that I be allowed to stay here until the case is concluded." Judge Dunne rejected his request; the court bailiffs led him from the courtroom, and he was booked into the county jail. Defense attorney Coghlan finished the closing arguments for both Frank and Albert. After defense attorney Hallinan bailed out of jail, he tried to return, but Judge Dunne refused to allow him in the courtroom.

The jury's first vote was 11–1 for guilty of first-degree murder. It was almost midnight before they were released for the night and returned to the hotel where they had been sequestered during the entire trial.

The jury deliberated all day Saturday and Sunday, and finally, on Monday, they reached a verdict of guilty of first-degree murder for both Frank and Albert. Frank was overheard telling his wife, "We're not licked yet dear." As reporters clamored to get a statement, Frank simply said, "We have nothing to say" before quickly adding, "I'm just beginning to fight."

Following the verdict, the public demanded more information about how the police listened in on conversations between Frank and Dr. Housman. The police admitted they placed a dictagraph machine after the gangland murder of Earl Leter. They explained they hoped to be able to solve Earl's murder by gleaning information. Instead, they said, they listened as Frank spoke of murdering Mrs. Hughes.

Captain Dullea explained to the reporters he tried to warn Mrs. Hughes that her life was in danger. He told reporters she shrugged off the information saying, "Why, my boy Frank would never hurt me." Captain Dullea said, over a period of time, he continued to warn her, but each time she denied such a thing could happen. He recalled that she said she was going to inform Frank about his warnings.

When the reporters inquired why the dictagraph evidence was not presented at the trial, Prosecutor Golden simply said it was not needed. Both defense attorneys stated the dictagraph evidence would not change their plans to request a new trial.

When asked by reporters about the evidence, Frank said: "If Captain Dullea had the slightest information ahead of time that there were plans afoot to commit a felony, it was his business to prevent it and not wait until it happened. They should have gone out to Dr. Housman's office, crashed into the place and arrested everybody in there in time to prevent the crime."[8]

Albert concurred saying, "Why didn't they bring out this information at the first trial if it is true? This looks like another frame on me-just like the gun charge. Why didn't they tail me when I got out of Folsom?"

After several delays, the day came when Frank and Albert returned to Judge Dunne's courtroom for sentencing. Both Frank and Albert were sentenced to life in prison. Frank walked through the gates of San Quentin prison and became inmate number 52917. Once inside the prison walls, he recognized Warden James Holohan and Guard Robert Curtain, both of whom he knew on a personal basis. Frank merely stated, "I want to conform to all the rules here and cause you no trouble." He spoke of himself in the third person when answering questions posed by reporters. "If Jessie Scott Hughes were alive, she would tell you that Frank Egan is innocent—that Frank Egan never would directly seek to harm her, or indirectly."

In a later interview, Frank told reporters: "I never thought I would come to this. This is terrible. Imagine going to prison as a murderer. In my worst nightmare nothing so awful as that ever happened. I can't realize it even yet."

Frank told reporters he withdrew his appeal so as to not cause his family any further financial grief. He denied his decision had anything to do with his fear that a new jury could vote for the death penalty. Upon hearing Frank's decision, Albert told reporters:

> Now, I do want to leave Mr. Egan out of this situation. Quite naturally I do feel grateful to him for withdrawing his appeal and giving me a chance to make a lone go of it for a new trial, but to say so publicly might make it appear to him that I am inclined to blame my being convicted on him.

> Mr. Egan knows I am innocent and I know he is. In my opinion he was not convicted according to law; he was convicted by public opinion. Truth was distorted. There were certain facts that hurt my chances, and I know Mr. Egan, in the face of the garbled truth, worried over the way they involved me.[9]

Verne pled guilty to a count of manslaughter, and Judge Dunne sentenced him to fifteen years in prison. Judge Dunne told the court: "Without Doran's testimony, Egan the master criminal, would not have been convicted." The judge expressed concern about Verne's safety at San Quentin:

> What of the boy's future in prison? Can't some protection be given him so that no hurt nor harm will befall him while he is serving sentence? There is some criticism due a community that allows a young man to be led astray by such as Egan. In large measure, Doran has expiated his crime. These people, Tinnin and Egan, according to information reaching me, are responsible for many other crimes and if they had not been stopped, they would have gone on.[10]

Weeks later, Dr. Housman was arrested on a charge of violating the state narcotics act. Dr. Housman vehemently denied any involvement and told reporters:

> It's all a frameup. It's a case of persecution on the part of the police and the newspapers, who have been hounding me right along. I don't know what this charge is all about. All I can think it might be is one case where I administered an opiate for some prisoner in the county jail and neglected to report the incident as required by law. But talk of me being connected with any "dope ring" or dope peddlers is a lot of bunk. I am being persecuted.[11]

Joseph Anderson of the State Narcotics Bureau had a different opinion on the matter:

> For more than two years Dr. Housman has been prescribing morphine, opium, and other drugs to patients who are apparently addicts, and has failed to report his prescriptions to the state division, required by law. He has issued hundreds of such prescriptions to a dozen patients—some of whom are very prominent.[12]

Verne was released from prison after serving two years. As he left the prison with $2.12 in his pocket, he reflected on the situation that got him into prison in the first place: "Frank Egan is guilty.... What's more I'd do it again. Frank ran out on me when I needed him most. If he and his boys had played ball with me Egan would never have been convicted. But they tried to run me into the river and I beat them to the punch."

When reporters from *The San Francisco Examiner* asked about his future plans, Verne told them: "I'm keeping out of trouble from now on. I've been studying in prison. Mathematics, radio engineering. Books of all kinds. I'll get by all right. I'm going to sea, and I'm going to stay there. If I can keep away from people like the birds that got me into trouble in the first place I'll be O.K."[13]

When Frank learned Verne had walked out of prison after two years, he irately told reporters from *The San Francisco Examiner*: "I will say little about Doran. Nothing will happen to him tomorrow. Verne Doran is the tool of my persecutors, but don't forget, I still have plenty of friends on the outside. And the only thing that permits me to carry on is that I know that I will be cleared and turned loose very soon now."[14]

Dr. Housman was never charged as an accomplice in the Frank Egan case, but he found himself back in court a few years later. Mignon Baker filed a lawsuit alleging Dr. Housman took advantage of a situation after her husband died. Mignon's husband, Lewis, was badly injured in an automobile accident and rushed to a hospital where he succumbed to his injuries. At the time he was admitted to the hospital, he had $9,874 in his possession.

The lawsuit alleged a friend of Dr. Housman's, John Farrell, who was also friends of the Bakers, authorized giving $5,000 to Dr. Housman for his services. Dr. Housman told the court: "Baker told Farrell to give me $5,000. I left Baker's side during his illness only to get coffee, or change my clothes. He had the severest skull fracture I ever saw. If I'd known that I would work four days and nights without rest I'd have demanded $10,000."

The surgeon who performed a two-hour operation on Lewis' brain, testified, "My fee was $500. That included the payment for the consultant work done by Dr. Howard Naffziger. Dr. Housman did no more than I did."

Superior Court Judge J. J. Trabucco ordered Dr. Housman to pay Mignon $2,500, and John was ordered to pay Mignon $3,000.

Shortly after Alma Elizabeth Black died in 1939, her relatives filed a lawsuit claiming Dr. Housman kept her under the influence of narcotics for seventeen years and influenced her to make him her sole heir. At stake was her estate valued at between $35,000 and $100,000. A settlement was reached between the heirs and Dr. Housman.

From the publicity surrounding the contested will, state agents from both the State Medical Board and the State Division of Narcotic Enforcement opened an investigation into Dr. Housman. They brought charges against Dr. Housman for failing to report narcotics that he prescribed. Dr. Housman's attorney said all records were meticulously kept and the officials were harassing his client.

The chief of the State Narcotics Bureau, Paul Madden, explained to the media: "At one pharmacy on Eddy Street, our agents found 345 prescriptions made out by Dr. Housman for more than 200 different patients. A check of our records disclosed that only four of these had been made known to our office. That is an intolerable situation."

The State Division of Narcotic Enforcement issued two arrest warrants for Dr. Housman. He surrendered at the jail and was soon released on bail. Weeks later, a trial got underway for the first two counts of charges against Dr. Housman for failing to properly document all narcotics that he prescribed. He was represented by defense attorneys John Taaffe and William Ferriter. Defense attorney Ferriter continually blamed the media for covering Alma's contested will, which he believed was the only reason Dr. Housman was under investigation.

The jury of eleven men and one woman learned that Alma's autopsy revealed she did not have the disease that Dr. Housman had been treating her with narcotics for the past seventeen years. The jury acquitted Dr. Housman on two charges, but he still faced thirty more charges. Additionally, felony charges for perjury, preparing false evidence, and offering false evidence were brought against Dr. Housman. An expert on handwriting testified that Dr. Housman's records had been tampered with, including an attempt to "age" the records by applying a chemical to the paper. An agent with the State Division of Narcotic Enforcement told the jury when he was at the Lewin Pharmacy, investigating Dr. Housman's records, he witnessed the doctor writing out copies of his records.

The next trial got underway with defense attorney Nathan Coghlan, who previously represented Albert Tinnin, defending Dr. Housman.

Inspector Walter Creighton of the State Division of Narcotics Enforcement testified: "I asked Doctor Housman several times for the records, and each time Doctor Housman said he had none. He said he didn't know he was supposed to keep them." The jury convicted Dr. Housman on three counts. He was sentenced to ninety days in jail and fined $750. His medical license was revoked. Dr. Housman was also found guilty of six counts of perjury stemming from the first trial and sentenced to one to fourteen years in prison.

Dr. Housman appealed his case to the U.S. Supreme Court and also asked the governor for a pardon. Neither of his requests were granted, and he entered San Quentin prison and was assigned to work in the mess hall. Dr. Housman was paroled after serving eighteen months. The State Board of Medical Examiners denied his petition to have his medical license reinstated. Dr. Housman died ten years after being paroled. He was fifty-five years old.

All of Frank's appeals were denied, and he remained in prison for twenty-five years to the day. For a period of time, the prison officials transferred Frank to Folsom prison after they tired of him providing legal advice to his fellow inmates. He returned to San Quentin which is where he was released from in 1957. Lorraine remained in contact with Frank during his years in prison, but she died several years before he was released. Frank died in 1961, at the age of seventy-nine.

5

Thomas and Burmah White

Burmah Arline Adams and Thomas White exchanged vows on September 1, 1933 in the living room at Burmah's parent's house in Santa Ana. Burmah wore a black satin dress with a matching hat and carried a bouquet of gardenias. Several friends of the family joined Burmah's parents in welcoming the new couple.

Burmah was nineteen years old and had recently moved to Los Angeles and began working at a beauty shop. Thomas, age thirty-one, told Burmah's family he was a stockbroker and had to get up at 5:30 each morning to check the first market reports from New York. He explained he lost an eye in an automobile accident. Thomas told Burmah and her parents that he inherited enough money to live comfortably for the next three years. What Thomas failed to mention was that he was wanted by the police, was known as the "Rattlesnake Bandit," lost his eye in a prison brawl, had spent his $1,000 inheritance in a matter of weeks, and had recently been paroled after a three-year stint in Folsom prison for thievery.

Shortly after the wedding, the police were called to a robbery in Los Angeles. The suspects described as a man and a woman were long gone, but a witness had written down the license plate of a car the police believed was involved in the robbery. The witness recalled seeing a male driving the vehicle with a female as the passenger. The next day, the police spotted the female driving the car and followed her as she drove to an automotive shop where she requested a new battery. Two police detectives donned mechanics' overalls and waited for the female to return and pick up the vehicle. When she did return, the detectives trailed her to a nearby apartment complex and watched as she went into a second-story apartment. Thomas came out of the apartment, saw the detectives, and immediately opened fire while standing in the stairwell. The gunfire was immediately returned by the detectives and Thomas fell to the ground fatally wounded. As the police approached Burmah, she tried to jump out a second-story window, exclaiming, "He was my husband. If he's dead I don't want to live. We were married five days ago."

Burmah was taken into custody and charged with eleven felony counts of first-degree robbery and assault with a deadly weapon. She was booked into the Lincoln Heights jail. When Burmah was interviewed by the detectives, she adamantly denied any involvement, stating, "I'm not guilty until proven so."

Burmah's father hired defense attorney Donald McKay. Donald immediately assured the media that his client was not guilty:

> Public feeling in this case has run almost to hysteria. She certainly has a defense, and the case against her is not as black as some people have made it out to be. It is too early yet, of course, to say just what the defense will be. I want an opportunity to cross examine the witnesses against her-an opportunity that was denied me at the coroner's inquest yesterday.[1]

The police allowed victims into the mortuary in an attempt to identify Thomas as the man who was responsible for committing crimes against them. Outside, a crowd estimated to be in excess of 3,000 people waited in the hopes of getting first-hand news of a crime spree that terrorized the Wilshire District of Los Angeles.

Burmah's parents were shocked at the turn of events from when they hosted the couple's wedding. Her mother told reporters, "A girl who loved her family as much as Burmah did, could never have done the terrible things they accuse her of." She spoke of the care Thomas showed Burmah's eleven-year-old sister, Jo: "Tommy was so kind and gentle with Jo and with Burmah that I can't believe what I hear but I guess it must be true if he had a prison record, but..." At that point, she began to cry from the magnitude of the situation.

The coroner's inquest resulted in Thomas being found guilty and the police justified in shooting Thomas. "We find that the deceased, Thomas White, came to his death from gunshot wounds inflicted by Lieutenants Arthur Bergeron and Bert G. Anderson, police officers, in the performance of their duty. We find this to have been justifiable homicide and we highly commend the officers for their action in this case."[2]

The police were able to tie Thomas to twenty robberies in the weeks leading up to his death. One robbery in particular angered the public. Two weeks before the wedding, Thomas and Burmah robbed Cromble Allen and Cora Withington at gunpoint. Thomas fired his gun, injuring Cromble and causing permanent blindness to Cora. The public raised $12,672 for Cora's ongoing medical care. The public wrote more than 3,000 letters to the governor of California protesting the criminal justice system that previously released Thomas from Folsom prison.

Several of the victims identified Burmah as the woman who was with Thomas when he committed the crimes against them. Mrs. George Kelly identified Burmah when she was robbed of $200 on September 5, 1933. Mrs. Arthur Baker said Thomas and Burmah robbed her on September 1, 1933—the day the couple was married. Mr. McCurdy identified Thomas and Burmah as the couple who robbed him at the service station he owned on August 26, 1933. Mrs. Elma Fell of Huntington Park identified Thomas and Burmah as the couple who robbed her of her purse containing $350 and jewelry.

While in the county jail, Burmah told reporter Erskine Johnson of *The Californian* a brief history of her life:

> I suppose every "life story" should begin with the date of birth. Mine was January 9, 1914. I first saw the light of day in Cleveland, Ohio, and we—my father and mother and I—lived there until I was through kindergarten and the first grade. Then we moved to Indianapolis, and five years later we came to California.
>
> I went to Santa Ana High School, after a while, and stayed two years, with my daily schedule about as interesting and exciting as a congressional report. I would get up at a certain time, wash my face, brush my teeth, eat breakfast and go to school. Then in the afternoon I would study after school and at night go to bed early.
>
> I wasn't allowed to have any boyfriends, but I didn't know what I was missing at that time.
>
> When I was ready to enter my senior year, however, I decided I wasn't learning much in high school, and so I quit and went to a beauty culture school. About this time my father and mother weakened a little and let me go with boys. I could step out two nights a week, but I had to be home by 11 o'clock.
>
> Meanwhile I was bent on being the world's best beauty operator. The course in that school in Santa Ana usually took only six months, but I went for a year. I could do finger waves and manicures that were beautiful to behold.
>
> Then I graduated, got my diploma and everything, and then I went to Balboa Beach and opened a beauty shop.
>
> Finally, I got a boyfriend—or thought I did—a man I thought was swell. But he went away. I had sort of stalled off about marrying him, and he sort of got discouraged because he was broke and left without telling me.
>
> I felt bad at first, but time healed my broken heart and a girlfriend of mine named Betty and I came to Los Angeles. I suppose you would say we decided to try our fortune in the big city.
>
> We had $10 between us, and then that 10-spot dwindled down to 30 cents before we got on a street car one day and went to Hollywood and both got jobs in beauty shops.
>
> Incidentally, I blonded my hair the day before we went on this excursion. It has always seemed to me blonds get by better than brunets. And then I met Tom White.
>
> I'm not going to say where, although I've been asked that before. And it was just one of those things. I felt his strange attraction—you might say strange

power—right from the first. And so we were married. Too bad, isn't it? That I can't say: "And lived happily ever afterward..."³

After a week at the county jail, Burmah had a change of heart, and told the grand jury everything she knew about the crimes. She explained that she met Thomas nearly three months before he died in the shootout with the detectives. She said they met at a dance but at the time she did not know anything about his criminal past.

Burmah admitted she came to know about his past after he forced her to participate in several of the robberies. Burmah told the panel of jurists Thomas threatened her and reminded her she was equally responsible for the crimes they committed together. She also mentioned they frequently had "knockdown-and-drag-out fights."

The trial got underway in Judge Fletcher Bowron's court. The state of California was represented by Deputy District Attorney George Stahlman. Over Burmah's objections, Judge Bowron appointed defense attorneys Robert Wheeler and George Francis when it was announced her previous defense attorney was ill. The jury consisted of six men and six women. Burmah's parents were present in the courtroom every day.

Deputy District Attorney Stahlman referred to Burmah's claim that Thomas forced her to participate in the crime spree as "ridiculous." He further explained, "It is a feeble attempt to lie her way out of this jam she is in. Every movement of this defendant indicates she was an acting, willing, helpful partner of Thomas White in his bandit raids."

Burmah's defense attorneys honed in on Thomas' past criminal background. He blamed Thomas for Burmah's criminal actions, claiming she would never have committed the crimes, had it not been for Thomas.

Before the jury began their deliberations, Judge Bowron instructed them that "fear of death at some future time is not a legal excuse for committing a crime." The jury quickly returned a verdict of guilty on all counts. Prior to sentencing, Judge Bowron told Burmah: "This court is convinced, as was the jury, that this girl engaged in various robberies with her husband willingly." Judge Bowron went onto say:

> The court also has considered the defendant's background. She is 19 years of age and comes from a good home, with good, honest parents, but she deliberately entered a life of crime.
> In all the robbery cases against her the only thing in her favor was her youth, but the time is past for maudlin sympathy for youth in crime, for it is of record that most of the crime of this day are perpetrated by youths.⁴

Judge Bowron sentenced Burmah to thirty years to life in prison. On the morning Burmah was transferred from the jail to the newly opened Tehachapi State

Prison, she posed for reporters carrying a tennis racket. She expressed her relief at being in the outdoors:

> I've been in here so long that when I get out for a few minutes I want to expose as much of myself to the sunlight as I can.
>
> It's a dubious honor to be the first prisoner to go to the new prison from Los Angeles County. But I hold no bitterness whatever against those who figured in my arrest and conviction because I realize they had to do their duty.
>
> I understand I can play tennis, volleyball and basketball at the prison. And I want to learn German and Russian—I know some French and Spanish. I intend to make the best of prison life so that it won't "get me."[5]

Burmah concluded by saying, "Either prison beats me or I beat it and I intend to beat it."

Burmah's sentence was reduced to sixteen years. She was released after serving just over eight years in prison.

6
Floyd Woodward

Thomas "Tommy" C. Thomas and his wife, Blanche, moved to Monrovia in 1930. Tommy explained to anyone who asked that he retired after selling a hotel in San Francisco because he wanted a quiet life. His dreams of such gave way with a knock on his front door on September 21, 1940.

The man knocking on the door told Tommy he saw the "For Sale" sign and wanted to view the house and property. Tommy had just started showing the stranger the outside of the property when two more men showed up. In a heartbeat, they placed Tommy in handcuffs and told him they were arresting him on charges of murder, mail fraud, and larceny. As the police led Tommy to their waiting police car, they explained they had been looking for him for twenty years.

Tommy was still in shock when he arrived at the Monrovia police station where he admitted he was actually Floyd Woodward, age fifty-four. The case began on April 3, 1919, when Ed Mills was murdered in Atlanta, Georgia. It was two years before a witness came forward with information regarding the murder. The witness wanted to remain anonymous for fear of the syndicate that was running gambling operations in Atlanta. The police were aware that Floyd Woodward was the "kingpin" of all the gambling operations in Atlanta. The anonymous tipster informed the police that Floyd was responsible for Ed's murder. The police did a full investigation, and in 1919, Floyd was indicted for the murder of Ed Mills. Floyd was also indicted for swindling J. W. Hatcher of $12,000 as part of a fraudulent stock market scam.

The police also wanted Floyd for seventeen counts of larceny having to do with scams he allegedly perpetrated. The scams involved false stock market claims, fake horse-racing stakes, and run-of-the-mill schemes. Additionally, the U.S. Postal Inspector was investigating a $125,000 scam involving horse racing that took place through the mail service. The police were armed with arrest warrants, but Floyd was nowhere to be found. As it turned out, it would be twenty years before Floyd surfaced.

During Floyd's first court appearance before United States Commissioner David Head, he exclaimed: "I have nothing to fear, and I am entirely innocent." Floyd waived extradition and plans got underway to return him to the state he fled twenty years before.

Blanche, along with the rest of the community, was shocked at the turn of events. Blanche and Floyd had been married for eleven years and had a six-year-old daughter. Blanche taught Sunday school and was involved with their church. Floyd was active in the community and in his church. He frequently played golf at the Arrowhead Springs Country Club.

The police credited a newspaper reporter by the name of Robert Standish, age twenty-four, for locating the man that they had been pursuing for twenty years. Robert was in the habit of studying wanted posters whenever he came across one.

Months before, Robert was visiting Waterman Canyon and inquired about renting a cabin. The man in charge of the rental was not available, but Robert spoke to another man who asked him to return at a later time to speak to the rental agent. Something about the man clicked in Robert's mind, and he decided to take another look at the wanted poster when he returned to San Bernardino. Robert's second look at the wanted poster convinced him that the man he met at the cabin was the man on the wanted poster. Robert immediately contacted the local police, but when they arrived at the cabin, the man was nowhere to be found.

Working on the tip that Robert provided, the detectives began a complete investigation. Their investigation led them to Floyd in Monrovia. They learned he owned real estate and was currently involved in a speculative real estate deal.

When the police had enough information to determine that Tommy was, in fact, Floyd Woodward, they contacted U.S. Postal Inspector H. N. Graham in New York. He was in charge of the fraud and racket division and was in possession of the twenty-year-old file. Armed with the file, he flew to California to assist with the arrest. Following the arrest, he stayed on in California to conduct further investigations. He seized a trunk that belonged to Floyd. Within the trunk were documents pertaining to fraudulent horse racing, stock market scams, and gambling.

While Floyd was in jail waiting to be extradited to Fulton County, Georgia, he wrote a letter to the *Monrovia News-Post*. The letter read:

> May I use a few lines in your paper to express to my friends in Monrovia my sincere appreciation for the gratifying evidence of their confidence and faith in me and the friendly comfort extended by them to Mrs. Thomas.
>
> My heart is filled with gratitude for all my neighbors and friends, who are so nobly sustaining us during this time.
>
> Appreciating your kindness, I am, sincerely yours, T.C. Thomas.[1]

Floyd appeared before U.S. District Court Judge Robert Russell in Atlanta. He pled guilty to defrauding seven people for a total of $53,800 and using the U.S. mail service to conduct his fraudulent racetrack gambling operation. Judge Russell sentenced Floyd to two years and eight months in federal prison.

Upon Floyd's release from prison, he was immediately arrested by law enforcement in Georgia for the murder of Ed Mills in 1919. A jury trial was held in April 1943. The panel of jurists found Floyd guilty, and he was sentenced to life imprisonment.

Four years later, Floyd was paroled after the State Prison and Parole Board determined there was doubt "as to the prisoner's guilt of premeditated murder." They explained to the media:

> Now in view of the prisoner's advanced age and bad health, the questionable circumstances surrounding his conviction, the fact that he has been fully rehabilitated according to the California investigation, the board has this day made an exception to the parole rules and ordered his release.[2]

Floyd returned home to his wife and daughter in Monrovia.

7
Emma LeDoux

In March 1906, workers at the Southern Pacific Railroad Depot noticed a trunk sitting on a platform that had not been claimed. They figured someone would claim it, but when it was time to close the depot for the night, the trunk was still sitting on the platform. When an employee picked up the heavy trunk and placed it inside the building, he was overcome by a strong odor emitting from the trunk.

Captain Walker opened the trunk and was shocked to find a dead body. He sent for the police and the coroner who began an investigation into the identity of the victim. Their investigation led them to Jamestown where Constable Solari of Jamestown identified the body as Albert McVicar.

The investigation revealed Albert worked in the timber industry at the Rawhide Mine in Jamestown in Toulumne County. He was in the process of divorcing his wife, Emma. Further investigation showed that Emma married Eugene LeDoux before the divorce from Albert was granted.

The police learned that Emma was the person who shipped the trunk. The trunk was originally scheduled to be sent from Stockton to Jamestown. Emma later changed the request for the trunk to arrive at Martella instead. Emma made arrangements for her brother to pick up the trunk in Martella.

The investigators discovered that, days before, Albert and Emma checked into a motel in Stockton using an alias of A. N. McVicar and wife. The police believed the murder took place at the hotel.

The investigation showed that Emma arrived in San Francisco two days before the body was discovered. She checked into the Royal House on Ellis Street. She immediately wired a friend, Joseph Healy, and asked him to meet her at the Royal House. Employees of the Royal House saw the two of them together all weekend. Emma left San Francisco and took the Santa Fe train to Stockton.

The police arrested Joseph Healy in connection with the murder. They believed Emma was responsible for murdering her husband, but that Joseph assisted her with placing the body in the trunk. The police had a difficult time finding Emma, but finally located her in Antioch.

Deputy Sheriff Carlton Case and District Attorney C. W. Norton traveled to Antioch and arrested Emma on a charge of first-degree murder. They told reporters Emma joked and laughed on the train ride. Each time the train pulled into a station, there were crowds hoping to catch a glimpse of the woman they had read about in the newspapers. Once they arrived at the jail, the authorities had to fight their way through the crowd while holding onto Emma. Once inside the jail, Emma reportedly continued to make jokes.

Emma's mother, Mary Head, of Sutter Creek, took the train to visit Emma in the county jail. Mary arranged for an attorney who she knew, Charles Crocker, to represent Emma. Charles and Emma grew up together in Amador County. Charles arranged for H. R. McNoble to be co-counsel.

During Emma's first court appearance, she pled not guilty before a courtroom overflowing with spectators. Emma admitted to knowing about the murder but pinned the blame for the crime on a man with the last name of Miller, who the police believed was fictious. Emma explained:

We had all been drinking and McVicar and I were drunk. McVicar had lots of money and Joe Miller gave him carbonic acid. Then I don't know just what happened. Miller and I put the body in the trunk and sent it to the depot. I wanted to go right away to my mother at Jackson, but Miller would not let me. He made me go to San Francisco with him Saturday night and Sunday. Last night we left San Francisco with tickets for Stockton. At Richmond Miller left me and went back to San Francisco and I got off at Antioch.

I did not kill McVicar. He died after a quarrel with Miller. I went into the room and saw McVicar frothing at the mouth. He may have been given carbonic acid by Miller when I was out of the room.[1]

To further her point, Emma produced a bottle of carbonic acid that was not completely full. She also showed the judge a knife she claimed belonged to Joseph. Emma offered additional details of the crime: "Miller got all the money. I do not know how much there was, but he got it. After McVicar was dead I went out and bought the trunk. Yes, that's true. Then we went to the Southern Pacific station after he put the body in the trunk. I helped him do that."[2]

Joseph took the witness stand and explained that he had received a telegram from Emma requesting that he meet her at the Royal House:

I remained at the lodging house quite late Saturday night, and went back again Sunday. I was sitting in the ladies' parlor reading, when I happened to notice the story of the Stockton murder. I told her [Emma] it was a terrible thing. She was very cool and said, "Yes, it was."

Then I did not know it was McVicar who had been killed, so I asked her what had become of McVicar. She said he had died at Sonora and that McVicar's brother had shipped the body to Denver. She also told me McVicar had a $5000 insurance policy that had been made out to her as beneficiary, but said he had later had it transferred to his mother. She said that McVicar's brother had told her, however, that he would get her $5000 out of it.[3]

As the investigation continued, the detectives discovered Emma had been married twice before. Her second husband died under what the police deemed suspicious circumstances. The police believed Emma may have received a life insurance settlement, but they could not prove it. They did learn Emma worked in the red-light district in San Francisco.

The autopsy revealed Albert suffered bruises on his head. There was no indication of carbonic acid. There was, however, a large quantity of morphine present in the body. Coroner Dr. J. P. Hull found Albert to be in good health at the time of his death. It was his opinion the death was caused by a large quantity of morphine. His investigation revealed Albert had not been a user of morphine prior to this death.

The police learned Emma purchased a bottle of cyanide of potassium at the Baldwin Pharmacy in San Francisco. She signed for the purchase using the name Mrs. A. N. McVicar, Jamestown, California.

While Emma was waiting for her trial to begin, San Francisco experienced one of its worst disasters when an earthquake and fire struck on April 18, 1906. This created many delays in Emma's case.

Shortly before the trial began, Emma requested a new pair of shoes to wear during the trial. She specifically asked for the latest footwear being worn in France. The jail staff asked a local shoe store to bring two pairs of shoes to the jail for Emma to try. She selected the pair she wanted and wore those to court.

The trial finally opened with Judge Nutter presiding. District Attorney C. W. Norton represented the state of California. Emma was represented by defense attorneys Charles Crocker and C. H. Fairall. Defense attorney H. R. Noble resigned from the case prior to the start of the trial.

On the opening day of the trial, Emma wore a black dress and a black hat complete with a veil. The trial opened to a standing room of spectators cramming every inch of the courtroom. In their opening statements, the defense claimed Albert met his death by suicide. The prosecution contended Emma murdered Albert in fear that her new husband, Eugene LeDoux, would discover she was still legally married to Albert.

The jury heard from autopsy surgeons, Dr. C. E. Letta and Dr. Hull. They dispelled the defense attorney's theory of suicide. Dr. R. R. Rodgers, professor at a local university, testified Albert had a large amount of morphine in his system at the time of his death. It was his opinion that there was enough morphine in Albert's system to kill a dozen men. He stated there was also a small amount of chloral present in Albert's system. When questioned if Albert could have died from being placed in the trunk, Dr. Rodgers stated that it was possible to breath while in the trunk. To confirm this, he got into the trunk and remained there for forty minutes, all the while carrying on a conversation.

Employees of the railroad testified they saw Albert and Emma traveling by train from Jamestown to Stockton. The jury listened to an employee of Breuner's Store describe how Emma purchased a large trunk from them on the day the murder occurred. They also heard from Frank LeDoux, Eugene's brother. He read letters allegedly written by Emma to Eugene while she was still married to Albert. In the letters, Emma proclaimed her love for Eugene. The jury learned Emma purchased morphine from a drugstore eleven days before Albert's death.

On the last day of testimony, Emma's mother, Mary, took the witness stand on her daughter's behalf. She admitted Emma had used morphine for at least four years and had used the drug while in jail, shortly before her trial began. It was Mary's testimony that Albert and Emma were legally divorced, but Albert had mentioned to her that he wanted to re-marry Emma.

Sheriff Sibley, the jail deputies, and jail matron Mrs. Benjamin all testified Emma did not have morphine with her at the jail.

During closing arguments, the prosecution stated: "She killed this man. She is guilty beyond a reasonable doubt and to a moral certainty. She committed the deed to protect herself from other crimes-from bigamy. She conceived, she planned, she encompassed the death of Albert N. McVicar, her lawful husband."[4] Hearing those words, Emma displayed emotions for the first time as she openly wept.

Finally, it was time for the jury of twelve men to deliberate. The spectators in the courtroom stayed put, fearing they would lose their seats if they left even for a minute. Outside on the courthouse lawn, crowds of people waited for the verdict.

It took the jury six hours to return a verdict of guilty of murder on the first degree. The jury did not recommend mercy, meaning Emma would be sentenced to hang for the murder of Albert. Hearing the verdict, Emma simply smiled and was led back to her jail cell. Mary chose not to be in the courtroom when the verdict was read. She waited outside and spoke briefly to Emma as she was being led back to the jail.

A reporter asked Emma if she wanted to say anything. She simply replied, "I don't know what I can say to you. I haven't anything to say. I can't say anything." With that, the magnitude of the situation hit her, and Emma began to sob.

During the trial, the jail staff and the sheriff assured the jury that Emma did not have any morphine in her jail cell. The day after learning of the verdict, Emma turned over her stash of morphine to the jail staff.

Emma was the first female to legally be sentenced to hang through the court system. Other females had been hung prior to this case, but they had not had the benefit of a court trial.

Judge Nutter set the execution date as October 19, 1906, but he granted Emma's defense team two months to file an appeal. Two months turned into two years as the appeal process dragged on. At one point, a reporter with the *Jamestown Magazine* asked Emma if she was hopeful of the appeal process. She quickly replied, "Why, I never worry—of course I have hopes—while there is life there is hope."

The 1,161-page appeal was accepted by the State Supreme Court in 1909. The State Supreme Court rejected the jury's verdict and ordered a new trial. Weeks before the new trial was to begin, Emma pled guilty to murder. Her attorney pleaded for a light sentence invoking biblical stories which resulted in Emma sobbing uncontrollably and placing her head on the defendant's table. Judge Nutter was not moved and sentenced Emma to life in prison. Emma was transferred to San Quentin prison.

Over the next few years, Emma's request for clemency and parole were denied. In 1920, Emma was paroled but her freedom was short lived. The following year, Emma found herself back in San Quentin prison after being arrested for operating a house of prostitution.

Emma remained in San Quentin prison for five more years before being granted parole once again. Soon after her release, her parole was revoked after it was determined she was involved with prostitution. Emma was returned to San Quentin prison before being transferred to the new Tehachapi Institute for Women prison when it opened. Emma's repeated requests for parole were denied. In 1941, Emma died in prison. She was sixty-nine years old.

8

The Mysterious Death of Thelma Todd

Shockwaves were felt throughout the tightly knit Hollywood community when thirty-year-old Thelma Todd was found dead in her automobile on the morning of December 16, 1935.

Thelma's maid, Mae Whitehead, found Thelma in the driver's seat of her car in the garage of her friend, Roland West, on Pasetano Road in Pacific Palisades. When the police arrived, the automobile was still running in the closed garage. At first glance, it appeared that the well-known actress committed suicide by carbon monoxide.

Thelma was wearing expensive jewelry and a mauve and silver evening gown underneath her mink coat. Her purse was in the car and did not appear that anyone had rifled through it. There was blood on her face, but the police believed that may have been caused when her body slumped over and hit the steering wheel.

Detectives arrived on scene and began piecing together the final hours of Thelma's life. They learned the previous evening she had attended a party hosted by Stanley and Ida Lupino at the Trocadero Cocktail Lounge. Thelma took a limousine home after the party but was unable to locate her apartment key. The detectives believed she went to the nearby home of her friend Roland West, where she kept her car, figuring she would wait until morning to ask anyone for help getting into her apartment. They figured she started the automobile so she could use the heater to stay warm.

Inside Thelma's apartment, the detectives located more than 100 wrapped Christmas presents, ready to be mailed. They did not notice anything suspicious or out of the ordinary.

Thelma was born and raised in Lawrence, Massachusetts. She obtained a teaching certificate from the Laurel Normal School and planned to become a schoolteacher. At the time she would have begun her teaching career, she had an opportunity to enter the Massachusetts Beauty Contest and to screen for a film. In a matter of days, she won "Miss Massachusetts" and was invited to join the

Paramount Pictures Players School in New York. After a short training period, Thelma appeared in her first film. She remained in New York for two years before moving to Hollywood.

Once in Hollywood, Thelma appeared in more than 100 films and was known for her starring roles in films and comedies. Shortly before her death, she signed a contract to star with Patsy Kelly in a series of comedy films for $1,500 per week.

Additionally, Thelma owned a café, "Thelma Todd's Sidewalk Café." The café was located at Roland's property. Thelma lived in an apartment above the café. The café was located on the road to Malibu Beach just north of Santa Monica. Thelma planned to expand the café to include a night club in the coming months.

In 1932, Thelma married Pasquale di Cicco at a small ceremony in Arizona. Soon after, they had a small church wedding in Los Angeles. After two years of marriage, Thelma filed for divorce citing Pasquale's cruelty and their incompatibility.

Thelma's mother, Alice, lived nearby, having moved to California to be close to her daughter. Her father, John, worked as a city representative in Lawrence. He died shortly after Thelma moved to Hollywood. Thelma's younger brother, William, died years before in an accident.

Upon learning of her daughter's death, Alice initially placed the blame on a heart ailment Thelma had recently learned about during a physical for an insurance policy. She then became increasingly vocal that Thelma's death was due to carbon monoxide poisoning: "My daughter's death was accidental. I am convinced of that. Suicide is entirely out of the question. She was too happy for that. Murder is unthinkable. She had no enemies who would wish to cause her death."

On the day of Thelma's funeral, thousands of people lined the streets leading to the church where a private service was held. Flowers were delivered from around the world. The public was allowed to view the open casket before Thelma was laid to rest at the Forest Lawn Memorial Park in a private ceremony attended by 200 guests. During the service, Thelma's pastor told those in attendance:

> As her pastor I wish to pay tribute to her genuineness. She was one of the most sincere persons I have ever been privileged to know. She was also one of the most honest persons I have ever dealt with. She was extremely congenial—at all times, the same sweet person.
>
> She was friend to all with whom she came in contact. She always recognized old friends under all circumstances. She was a great lover of children.
>
> She was very charitable. At Thanksgiving time I know that she packed, paid for and personally distributed thirty well-filled baskets to the needy. She had twenty-seven families on her Christmas list.[1]

Those who worked with Thelma remembered her as being friendly with every staff member on the movie set. One employee recalled: "If anyone on the lot of little means was injured or needed medical attention, Thelma always arranged it, and arranged it so that the person never knew whence came his help."

A co-worker of Thelma's gave an example of a young man who worked on the movie set who was in need of an operation. Thelma paid for the operation out of her own pocket anonymously.

Detectives interviewed the guests who attended the Lupinos' party. They also questioned the staff at the Trocadero Cocktail Lounge who worked the night of the party but did not come up with any answers.

The investigators learned that Pasquale attended the party at the Trocadero the night before Thelma's body was discovered. He informed the detectives he saw Thelma from across the room, but never spoke with her.

The driver of the limousine who drove Thelma home from the party told the detectives he dropped Thelma off at her apartment at approximately 2 a.m. He recalled Thelma saying she had an appointment at 1:55 a.m., but he did not have any further details. He said on previous occasions when he drove her home, he recalled seeing Roland outside waiting for her, but he did not see him on the morning of December 16.

The detectives questioned Roland West. When asked why Thelma would not have woken him when she realized she was locked out of her apartment, he stated she was too considerate to wake anyone at 2 a.m.

During a subsequent interview, Roland admitted to the detectives he locked Thelma out of her apartment the night of the party. Roland directed many of the films Thelma starred in. He was well known in Hollywood for producing and directing films. Six years prior to Thelma's death, he produced the movie *Alibi*.

Thelma's café manager, Rudolph Schafer, was Roland's brother-in-law. He told the police he had been out of town for eight days, arriving home the day before Thelma's body was discovered inside her automobile. He assured the police the café was doing well financially, and Thelma was excited about the expansion.

Martha Ford told the detectives she received a phone call from Thelma confirming she planned to attend the party the Fords were hosting the night of December 16. According to Martha, Thelma accepted the invitation and was looking forward to attending. Martha told the detectives Thelma mentioned she would be bringing her new boyfriend.

The detectives were busy running down leads, including one that said Thelma was assaulted at the café days before her body was discovered. An anonymous source told the police Thelma was overheard arguing with a man, who then struck her and knocked her across a table.

The detectives learned two men had been arrested in New York for attempting to extort $10,000 from Thelma. Thelma received the extortion notes earlier in the year. The letters were written in pencil on plain white paper and signed "Ace of Hearts." The notes were postmarked in New York. One note threatened to blow up the café if the money was not paid. Another note threatened "death and mutilation." The extortion notes rattled Thelma enough that she hired a bodyguard for a period of time. One of the men arrested was committed to the Bellevue State Hospital in New York, the other was under indictment at the time Thelma died.

A grand jury was convened to determine if Thelma was murdered by carbon monoxide, committed suicide, or died by accidental carbon monoxide poisoning. The courthouse took on the appearance of a movie set with many of Hollywood's leading actors and actresses lining the halls of the courthouse waiting to be called to testify.

Ida testified listening to Thelma talk about the new man in her life while they were at the Lupino's party at the Trocadero Cocktail Lounge. She recalled Thelma saying: "I'm in the midst of the most marvelous romance I've ever had, with a San Francisco business man who is just too grand for words."

Ida told the grand jury that the fact that Pasquale was at the Trocadero was not a coincidence. Ida explained he had telephoned her after learning about the party and asked why he had not been invited. Ida said she told him she did not think it would be a good idea for him to attend, but he insisted. The night of the party, Ida said, they saved a chair for him at the table, but he never came to the table. Instead, he was seen across the room with his girlfriend, Margaret Lindsay.

The District Attorney's Office ordered a complete investigation into the identity of the man Thelma mentioned to Ida that lived in San Francisco. After a thorough investigation, they were not able to locate the man.

Roland's estranged wife, Jewell, testified she saw Thelma driving on Hollywood Boulevard with a male passenger the night before her body was discovered. She described the male as a "handsome foreigner."

A friend of Thelma's, Duke York, Jr., testified that he was the man Thelma planned to bring to the Ford's party. He claimed he did not come forward sooner because "there seemed no point in adding to all the rumors that were making publicity out of the case."

Roland appeared before the grand jury and explained that he did lock Thelma out of her apartment. The jurors asked many questions, but Roland's only explanation was that it was a "misunderstanding."

Erwin Luttermoser, a certified public accountant, gave an overview of the Thelma Todd's Sidewalk Café's finances. His testimony did not give a clear picture as to if the café was experiencing financial problems.

Rudolph testified for more than an hour. The jurors questioned him about the café's finances and Thelma's relationship with Roland. He stated he did not know anything about her personal life. He denied knowing that Thelma was assaulted at the café.

Pasquale left for New York soon after Thelma's death. The grand jury subpoenaed him to return to California and appear before them. He emphatically stated, "I have no idea how Thelma died." He conceded the possibility that

Thelma was murdered. He went onto say: "Thelma and I were completely separated. There had been no possibility of a reconciliation and re-marriage."

The grand jury requested to be taken to the crime scene. They walked the steep grounds, and some members climbed the 271 steps from the café up to Thelma's apartment. They came away with doubts that Thelma could have negotiated the steep climb in the dark, wearing an evening gown, a full-length fur coat, and the thin-soled shoes she was wearing when her body was discovered. The jury ate lunch at Thelma Todd's Sidewalk Café where Roland served as their host. The jurors were left with more questions than answers when they left the crime scene.

After a parade of witnesses appeared before the grand jury, the foreman of the jury announced: "It is obvious that certain witnesses either have concealed things they know, or have given false evidence." He went onto say that a portion of the grand jury was convinced Thelma was murdered, but they were frustrated in not having concrete evidence.

After three weeks of hearing testimony, the grand jury announced they were at an impasse and the investigation was officially closed as an accidental death.

Thelma's pastor once said in describing Thelma's death, "Life is full of mystery and unexpected events." Nearly 100 years later, the mystery remains as to the cause of Thelma's death.

9
Arthur Eggers

When a headless and handless torso was found on January 2, 1946 in a remote spot in a canyon off the Rim of the World Highway in the San Bernardino mountains, the police opened an investigation. There were two bullet holes in the torso; one of which was directly through the heart. The detectives checked their missing persons list and noted that Arthur Eggers, age fifty-two, had reported his wife, Dorothy, missing the same day that the torso was located.

Years before, Arthur's father served as the sheriff of San Francisco County and worked as a city supervisor in San Francisco. Arthur worked as a clerk in the Temple City Sheriff's Substation and had been employed there for seventeen years. He fell under suspicion after reporting his wife missing. The deputies felt something was off when they asked him casual questions about his wife's disappearance. His answers were not consistent and seemed evasive. At one point, Arthur told several deputies he had viewed the torso in the basement of the sheriff's office, and concluded it was not his wife. This further aroused the deputies' suspicions, as the torso had never been in the basement, but instead was being held at a local mortuary.

The detectives went to Arthur's home in Temple City to gather additional information. They questioned Dorothy and Arthur's daughters, ages nineteen and eleven, regarding Dorothy's disappearance. The detectives showed both girls a blanket the torso had been wrapped in. The younger daughter identified the blanket as one that belonged to their mother. The older daughter denied the blanket belonged to her mother. When Arthur learned his younger daughter identified the blanket, he immediately accused her of lying.

Arthur was taken to the San Bernardino Sheriff's Office for further questioning. He was questioned by Los Angeles County Sheriff Eugene Biscailuz and San Bernardino Sheriff Emmett Shay.

During the interview with the sheriffs, they informed Arthur the torso held two bullets from a .38 automatic weapon. Arthur admitted at one time he owned a .38 automatic weapon, but he insisted he had sold it. Arthur told the detectives he and Dorothy had argued about finances four days before he reported her missing. He mentioned the night following the argument he got in his car "and drove all night, going as far as Long Beach."

Arthur told the detectives Dorothy frequently had men at their house when he was at work. He told of seeing a man leaving their house when he arrived home days before Dorothy disappeared. It was his belief that one of Dorothy's men had killed her or that she had picked up a hitchhiker who murdered her and left her dismembered body in the canyon. Arthur further explained: "After she disappeared, the girls told me he had been to the house on two occasions in December. I wasn't there, I was working and I didn't see him, but the girls did. I asked the girls where he lived and they said in Arizona."

The Eggers' eleven-year-old daughter told the detectives, "Daddy kept telling me over and over, that I had seen Mama in bed—but I hadn't." She was referring to the night Dorothy disappeared.

A subsequent search of the Eggers' home revealed human bloodstains in the bathroom. Police Chemist Ray Pinker was able to match strands of hair in the Eggers' bathroom to the strands of hair located on the blanket that the torso was wrapped in. During the search of the house, it became apparent that all of Dorothy's clothes were missing. Arthur explained that he gave her clothes away after she disappeared. Arthur was asked about the clothing found in his house with bloodstains. He replied: "I don't believe there were any clothes found in my house with blood stains on them. If there were any with blood stains on them I would have washed them off."

In the days following Dorothy's disappearance, Arthur sold her car to a deputy at work. When the deputy opened the trunk of the car, he could tell the bottom of the trunk had recently been repainted. When he examined it further, he noticed stains on the bottom of the trunk. He had those stains analyzed and they were determined to be human blood.

Arthur was arrested and booked into the county jail on a charge of suspicion of murder. He identified the torso as that of his wife saying, "I'd say that was her. I'll claim the body."

Arthur continued to deny any involvement with his wife's disappearance. He told the detectives there was a soldier serving in India that had taken his wife out while they were married and corresponded with her when he was in India. He expanded by saying, "She went out with other men. I knew it but I think she felt she could control men. She must have met someone she couldn't control."

After five days in jail, Arthur provided Captain Gordon Bowers with a full confession. Although Arthur had continuously said he "wouldn't harm a hair on my wife's head," he now offered an entire confession. Arthur admitted to murdering his wife of nineteen years. He said he dismembered the body in the hopes it would not be possible to identify it. He admitted he tossed the torso in a ravine near the Rim of the World. Arthur clarified his actions by saying:

> I drove through San Bernardino between 2 and 2:30 a.m. on Sunday. It was December 30. I started up the road to the mountains. It was very foggy and I was driving slow. I had only gone a mile or so when I pulled over to the side and rolled the body down a canyon. Then I got in the car again and drove on about four or five miles. There I threw the head and hands down another canyon. I had them in a cardboard carton. I didn't open the carton but just pitched it out of the car.
>
> It seemed to me to be four or five miles from where I threw out the body, but I was driving slow and it may not have been quite so far. All the time I was looking for a likely canyon and that one seemed the first I had found. The road was wide there, so wide I could make a full turn around without backing the car.[1]

Arthur told Sheriff Shay that he felt better after telling the truth. He apologized to Captain Bowers for having "held out so long." Arthur explained, "I was frightened, and ashamed, and I didn't know what to do at first."

Arthur was taken by vehicle to try and find the head and hands that he threw out his car window. Sheriff deputies in nine vehicles followed behind the car Arthur was in to search every ravine. In addition to the missing body parts, they were also searching for a firearm and a saw Arthur said he tossed out his car window. The search continued for days, but nothing was ever found.

Arthur answered additional questions as to how the murder took place. He responded by saying he and Dorothy had an argument after he accused her of having an affair. She did not deny being unfaithful, according to Arthur, and even told him she planned to continue to see other men. Arthur said it was then he pushed her down and struck her. He said when she got up, he went to grab his firearm and ran after her. Arthur told Sheriff Biscailuz, "I was never so mad—crazy mad. I shot her. When she fell into the bathtub, I shot her again."

Arthur said once he knew for sure Dorothy was actually dead, he decided to "cut her to pieces and scatter the pieces along the highways—anywhere." He recalled for the sheriff how he wrapped the body in a blanket and carried it out to the car. He said he placed the body in the trunk and proceeded to saw the head and neck off. When he finished that, Arthur said he sawed Dorothy's hands off. When asked to explain, Arthur said, "I wasn't trying to hide her identity. I didn't care. I was going to cut her to pieces."

Sheriff Biscailuz asked Arthur further questions about where he disposed of the body, the firearm, and the saw. In response, he replied:

> I didn't know where I was going. Somewhere—just anywhere. I drove to Fish Canyon, near Azusa. There I threw away my pistol and the saw. Then I returned to the highway and drove—drove for an hour it seemed. I decided to throw the body, head, and hands into a canyon. I had heard of the San Bernardino mountains. I drove through San Bernardino and north toward the mountains.

> It was dark and foggy in the mountains. I stopped at what I thought was the first likely place, lifted the body out and hurled it over an embankment into a ravine. Then I drove on, four or five miles, it seemed. It was so foggy that I could hardly see the road. Then I came to a stone wall along the edge of the canyon. I stopped, took the carton out of the car and stepped up to the wall. I threw it—with both hands—just as far as I could.[2]

Arthur said he then drove home. He recalled washing the bathroom floor before going to bed. When asked if he slept well, Arthur assured the sheriff he slept fine because he was tired. He told the sheriff he believed his daughters slept through the shouting and the murder.

When the detectives questioned Arthur further about the possible location where he said he tossed the body parts out of his car window, he changed his story. He apologized: "I thought you would just glance around the canyon and failing in your search, would call it quits. I'm sorry." He then said, "I burned the head and hands in my incinerator."

Sheriff Biscailuz replied: "You cannot build a fire hot enough to destroy a human skull in a home incinerator." Arthur angrily said: "Oh, yes I did. I used papers and wooden boxes. They made a hot fire." He explained that he kept the fire going for three days. He went onto say he scattered the ashes in his yard and burying the pieces of bone that did not burn. In anticipation of Sheriff Biscailuz' disbelief, Arthur quickly added: "Well, I'm telling the truth now."

Arthur was formally charged with first-degree murder. Arthur admitted to forging Dorothy's name on the title transfer of Dorothy's car. A felony charge of grand theft was added. Arthur pled not guilty to the murder charge, but then changed his plea to not guilty by reason of insanity.

A jury of ten women and two men found Arthur guilty of first-degree murder. During the trial, Arthur admitted to shooting his wife but denied cutting her head and hands off. When he heard the verdict, he turned to his attorney, James Starritt, and exclaimed, "How could they? That was not Dorothy's body." Another trial was held to determine if in fact Arthur was insane at the time of the murder. During the trial, Arthur denied killing his wife and explained that after they had an argument about Dorothy's infidelity, he got in his car and went for a drive. The jury returned a verdict of sane. The jury did not recommend leniency and Arthur was placed on death row at San Quentin prison.

The State Supreme Court upheld the decision of the court and the U.S. Supreme Court refused to hear the case. Acting California Governor Goodwin Knight denied a stay of execution. An execution date was set and on the morning of October 16, 1948 Arthur was put to death, all the while declaring, "I may have shot her, but I never cut her up."

10

Louise Peete

When Jacob Charles Denton's daughter, Frances, was not able to reach her father by telephone, an investigation was opened. Detective A. J. Cody was assigned the case. On September 23, 1920, Detective Cody and a private investigator, Rush Blodgett, went to Jacob's house on South Catalina Street in Los Angeles.

They entered the house and did not locate anything out of the ordinary until they came to a doorway at the end of a narrow hallway. The door led to a basement where they encountered a heavy door. The door was secured with two boards nailed across it. In front of the door there were stacks of boxes and trunks. Once they made their way past the door, they discovered a tiny room. The floor of the room was covered with a huge pile of dirt, newspapers, and canvas. Using a piece of wood, they located nearby, they used the piece of wood to scrap away at the pile of dirt. As they dug, they saw a piece of material. They continued to dig until they saw a decomposed body.

Detective Cady requested additional law enforcement who arrived a short time later. Together they carefully removed the material which turned out to be a quilt and saw a man's body. The body was wrapped in an old quilt with canvas on top. The body had five ropes tied tightly around the body. The hands and feet were tied with rope and there was a rope around the man's neck, and two around the middle of the body. The detective believed the ropes around the middle section were used to carry the body down to the basement. The man was wearing a white shirt, dark pants, white socks, and white tennis shoes. The ring on his finger was missing a diamond. He had been shot in the stomach.

While searching the house for evidence, the investigators located a small handgun hidden in a can of baking powder a few feet from the body.

The body was later identified as Jacob Charles Denton, age forty-six. The police opened an investigation and learned Jacob and his wife purchased the house on May 19, 1920. Jacob's wife died shortly thereafter from an illness. Jacob had been very successful in mining speculations in Arizona where he lived prior to moving to California. Jacob owned another house in Los Angeles, as well as properties in Missouri and Arizona. After Jacob's wife died, he advertised his house on South Catalina Street for rent with the condition he be allowed to remain in one room of the house.

The investigation revealed Louise Peete rented the house from Jacob who agreed to the stipulation that Jacob could remain in a small portion of the expansive house. Louise had recently moved from Denver, Colorado. She was married, but her husband, Richard, remained in Colorado with their five-year-old daughter, Betty.

The detectives began looking into Louise's background. They soon learned she was known to law enforcement in Boston, Massachusetts. According to Boston Police Captain Ainsley Armstrong, Louise Gould arrived in Boston in 1911, at the age of nineteen, and told people she was an heiress with properties in Norway and Germany. She roomed with a prominent family in Boston who treated her as a daughter. Louise opened credit accounts at many of Boston's best stores. When the stores became suspicious after not receiving any payments, Captain Armstrong questioned Louise. She admitted she had lied about her background and admitted to being an imposter. No charges were brought for fear of bad publicity and Louise was never charged with any crimes.

Louise's next encounter with the Boston Police Department was after she and her husband, Henry Bostley, moved next door to an elderly woman in Boston. Louise worked as the woman's caregiver. Soon after she began her employment, the woman's family noticed $20,000 of diamond jewelry was missing. The police recovered the diamond jewelry at Louise's house. The woman chose not to prosecute Louise so as to avoid any publicity. Henry later took his own life.

The detectives learned that in Dallas, Texas, an elderly woman, Mrs. Pierson, rented a room to Louise. Soon after Louise moved in, Mrs. Pierson told the police a $500 diamond was stolen from a piece of jewelry. The jewelry had been hidden inside a mattress. When the police tried to contact Louise to question her, they found her lying on her bed with a bottle of poison nearby. They discovered that despite the appearance that Louise had swallowed the poison, they saw that she had actually poured it down the sink. Louise claimed she gave the diamond to her husband, Harry Faurote. The police recovered the diamond and Mrs. Pierson declined to press charges. Harry was shot in Waco, Texas. The police classified it as a suicide, but Harry's family believed he was murdered. Soon after, Louise married Richard Peete in Denver.

The police learned Louise moved out of Jacob's house in August and rented it to a woman by the name of Mrs. Tilton before returning to Denver. She informed the police Louise rented the house to her for $300 a month. She stressed she had never been down to the basement and had no knowledge there was a body buried there. Mrs. Tilton said when Louise moved out, she gave her Jacob's bank books, notebooks, two watches, a suitcase full of personal papers, and some of his clothing. Mrs. Tilton showed the police a pawn slip, dated August 9, 1920.

Mrs. Tilton explained that Louise asked her to pawn a ring that belonged to Jacob.

The police in Denver made contact with Louise who expressed complete disbelief that Jacob had been murdered. She told the authorities she lived in Jacob's house for three months before returning to Denver. She said she returned to Los Angeles in July and saw Jacob briefly at that time. Louise said Jacob moved to Seattle and she lost touch with him.

Louise explained Jacob frequently had arguments with his relatives and she felt that was the reason he moved to Seattle. She also spoke of a woman she saw Jacob with at the house the night before he left for Seattle. She recalled hearing the two of them arguing.

Louise showed the police a copy of Jacob's will that she said she found in his desk. The will was dated May 15, 1920. The will was signed by Jacob, but not witnessed. An attorney representing Jacob, Judge Avery, told the police Jacob updated his final will two weeks before he disappeared. His reason, Judge Avery explained, was he feared something was going to happen to him.

A witness came forward and told the police the company he worked for sent him to deliver a load of dirt at Jacob's house on June 8, 1920. He recalled Louise telling him that Jacob was in Seattle. The investigators believed that Jacob was murdered on June 2, 1920 based on the fact he was last seen alive the previous day.

An investigation into Jacob's finances revealed two checks were written after Jacob was murdered. One check was written for $450, the other for $50. Both checks were made payable to Louise. When Louise was questioned about the checks, she quickly stated Jacob asked her to write the checks on his behalf because he had recently had his arm amputated.

The Los Angeles County Grand Jury indicted Louise for the murder of Jacob. District Attorney Thomas Woolwine issued an arrest warrant. The police located Louise and she was booked into the county jail. She pled not guilty to the charge of first-degree murder and a trial date was set.

The trial began in January 1921 with Superior Court Judge Frank Willis presiding. District Attorney Woolwine, Deputy District Attorney Raymond Turney, Robert Scott, and A. H. Van Cott represented the state of California. Louise was represented by public defender William Aggeler. Twelve men made up the jury. Louise's husband, Richard, sat next to her at the defense table every day.

The jury heard from James Crowhurst, who told of doing some plumbing work at Jacob's house. He said Louise would not allow him to go near the basement where Jacob's body was found. James told the jury when he was fixing the water heater in the house, she complained that the water heater was making noises that sounded like "graveyard groans." A gardener who did work at the house testified he lent a shovel to Louise in June.

After the jury heard from the law enforcement officers, the defense and prosecution presented their closing arguments. Over the course of three hours, the defense continually reminded the jury it was their duty to give Louise the benefit of reasonable doubt. He cautioned them of convicting an innocent person.

District Attorney Woolwine informed the jury, "I have never seen anything in my life equal to this defense. It is almost idiotic. That's their whole case. It doesn't amount to anything." Before turning the case over to the jury, he referred to Louise as the "most red-handed and brutal murderess ever known in this country."

After six ballots and five hours of deliberations, the twelve members of the jury reached a unanimous decision. They announced a verdict of guilty of first-degree murder with a recommendation of life imprisonment. Louise did not show any emotion as she was led out of the courtroom, but Richard was visibly shaken.

Richard brought their daughter to visit Louise in jail. He provided Louise with material, and she spent her days sewing and knitting items for her daughter. During their visits, Betty would play on the grass outside, while Louise looked on from her jail cell. A Los Angeles theater production company offered the Peetes money if they allowed Betty to be cast in a play billed as the "Daughter of Louise Peete, murderess of Jacob Charles Denton." The Peetes declined the offer. Later Louise was transferred to San Quentin Prison, then to Tehachapi State Prison. Richard committed suicide three years into Louise's prison stay.

Betty was a grown woman when Louise was granted parole in 1939 after eight previous denials for freedom. After serving eighteen years, Louise walked out of prison. She soon married Lee Judson.

Five years after walking out of prison, Louise found herself behind bars yet again. Louise and Lee were charged with murder on December 23, 1944.

When the body of a female was discovered in a shallow grave in Pacific Palisades in December 1944, the police opened an investigation. They discovered the victim was Margaret Logan, age sixty. She had suffered a gunshot wound and numerous blows to the head with a hammer.

The investigation led them to Louise. She was employed as a housekeeper for Margaret. As a condition of Louise's parole, her employer had to sign a form every month. The authorities became suspicious that the signatures were fraudulent and opened an investigation.

Once they spoke to Louise, she immediately claimed Margaret's husband, Arthur Logan, was responsible. Louise told the police: "While he was slapping her with the gun, it went off." Louise recalled: "Mr. Logan attacked his wife on several occasions, and even the day she filed the first sanity complaint against him, November 26, 1943, she had a black eye."

Louise described what happened the day Margaret was murdered. She said the three of them were preparing to leave the house when Margaret went back into the house to answer the telephone. Arthur followed Margaret and moments later, Louise said, Margaret began screaming for her. When she ran into the house, Arthur had his hands around Margaret's neck. It was Louise's statement that Arthur killed Margaret at that moment. Louise said she gave Arthur a tranquilizer and proceeded to dig a grave in the backyard: "I admit burying the body ... that's all I have to say now." She denied her husband had anything to do with the murder, adding that he did not know she had been convicted of murdering Jacob.

Louise said she and Lee took Arthur to the state mental hospital. She admitted to posing as his foster sister in order to admit him. She clarified that Arthur died in the state mental hospital before Margaret's body was discovered. Louise admitted she and Lee lived in the house from the time of the murder until their arrest. The police located a .32-caliber revolver in Louise's dresser at Margaret's house.

Margaret was last seen alive on June 1, 1944. Twenty-four years earlier, Jacob was last seen alive on June 1. Louise's reason for not reporting the crime when it occurred in June was that she believed her past would cast suspicions on her.

As the detectives continued their investigation into the murder of Margaret, they began investigating the death of Emily Latham. Emily worked as a parole officer and was instrumental in getting Louise released from prison. Louise worked as a caregiver to Emily. Louise admitted she assisted Emily in writing her last will days before she died. Soon after Louise moved into Emily's house, Emily died from a cerebral hemorrhage. The death was determined to be from natural causes.

The detectives learned that when Louise found herself out of a job at Emily's house, she went to work for Mrs. Marcy, age sixty. Mrs. Marcy was a neighbor of Emily's. She too died from natural causes, soon after Louise moved in. When Louise was questioned about the death, she told the police Mrs. Marcy took a bad fall and went to a hospital, where she died.

As the investigation continued, the detectives concluded that Lee was not involved with the murder. They released him from custody. Twenty hours after being released from jail, Lee committed suicide by leaping from a nine-story building in Los Angeles. Louise stated she was not going to attend Lee's funeral because she did not want to cause his family any grief.

Louise's trial began in May 1945 for the murder of Margaret with Superior Court Judge Harold Landreth presiding. Deputy District Attorney John Barnes represented the state of California. Louise was represented by public defenders William Neeley and Ellery Cuff. The jury was made up of eleven women and one man.

During the prosecution's opening statements, they informed the jury that Louise murdered Margaret to benefit financially. They also spoke of a heated argument between Margaret and Louise over a $200 check that Margaret claimed Louise forged. From the defense table, Louise shouted, "It's a lie!"

Police Chemist Roy Pinker testified Louise admitted to him she had forged Margaret's name on her parole papers because "Mrs. Logan did not want to be bothered." He also described recovering a .32-caliber bullet from the Logans' living room wall even though the wall had been plastered over. He explained to the panel of jurists that the bullet bore similar markings to the bullets he fired from the gun recovered from Louise's bedroom dresser. He showed the jury a section of the Logans' floor that had been stained with blood.

Dr. Jesse Carr, a pathologist with the University of California, informed the jury that Margaret suffered a gunshot wound. He went onto say she may have been alive when she was buried. He emphasized Margaret could have lived if she had had proper medical care after being shot.

All eyes were on Louise as she walked to the witness stand. She was dressed in a light blue suit with a black hat and veil. For those in the overflowing courtroom who expected to hear any new information, they were sorely disappointed. Louise adamantly denied any involvement in the murder, again placing the blame on Arthur. She did admit to burying the body in the Logans' backyard after spending hours digging a grave. Louise told of how angry Arthur would become over the slightest incident. She spoke of Arthur's faulty memory and general confusion.

The prosecution told the jury that Louise pretended to be Margaret in order to collect Arthur's insurance. They also said when Louise was asked about Margaret's whereabouts, Louise would say she was having plastic surgery to cover up the damage Arthur caused when he hit her.

A neighbor of the Logans', Edythe Fish, told the jury she received the telegram from the hospital notifying Margaret that Arthur had died. Edythe took the telegram to the Logans' house and gave it to Louise. She explained further: "I went into the house and handed the telegram to Louise. She read it and ran into the bedroom. She came out with several hats and started doing a little dance while trying them on. I stood there amazed at her reaction and she quieted down. She asked me not to get the impression that she was trying one on for Mr. Logan's funeral."[1]

Edythe also told of hearing "digging noises" coming from the Logans' backyard. Although she did not recall the exact date, she testified that it occurred between May 27 and June 18, 1944.

The defense and prosecution completed their closing arguments, and the jury began deliberating. While the jury was out deliberating, Louise spent her time reading a book titled *The Importance of Living*.

When the jury returned to the courtroom, it became apparent that Louise would not be able to put the book's message to use. The jury found Louise guilty of first-degree murder. The jury did not recommend leniency, meaning she would be executed. Once the jury was polled, Louise stood up and asked, "Is that all?" A deputy sheriff handcuffed her and led her out of the courtroom. As Louise passed a group of reporters, she thanked them for their kindness. When she noticed one female reporter seemed upset, Louise told her, "Don't weep for me dear."

When Louise arrived at the jail, she told the jail matron, "The verdict was inevitable. Halfway through the trial I was sure that it would be. It's too bad Mrs. Logan wasn't in the courtroom to see how unjust that verdict was."

Judge Landreth sentenced Louise to die in the gas chamber. Louise was never charged with any other murders. The State Supreme Court upheld the court's decision. The U.S. Supreme Court refused to review Louise's case. Her only hope lay with Governor Warren. She assured reporters that Governor Warren was a gentleman and "no gentleman would send a lady to her death."

Gentleman or not, Governor Warren declined to offer Louise clemency stating, "After carefully studying the records in the case of Mrs. Peete and communicating with public officials who knew the case thoroughly, I am of the opinion that the facts do not warrant any interference on my part with the judgment of the court."

Louise was transferred from Tehachapi State Prison to San Quentin prison. The night before Louise was scheduled to be executed, she gave a final interview to reporters. She emphasized: "I did not kill them I did not kill Denton. I did not kill Mrs. Logan. I forged Mrs. Logan's name; yes. But that is all…"

Louise ate fried chicken, avocado salad, and pumpkin pie for her last meal. She lay down on a prison cot with a dimly lit light bulb hanging overhead. Eight years to the day Louise was paroled after serving eighteen years for the murder of Jacob Denton, she faced her own execution. She put on a brown floral dress and walked with three jail matrons to the gas chamber. Eleven minutes later, Louise was pronounced dead. She was the second woman in California to die in the gas chamber.

11
Walburga "Dolly" Oesterreich

Just before midnight on the night of August 22, 1922 shots rang out at a house in Lafayette Park in Los Angeles. When the police arrived, they found Fred Oesterreich dead on the floor and his wife, Walburga "Dolly," locked in an upstairs bedroom closet. The door to the closet had been locked from the outside. Fred had been shot three times with a .25-caliber bullet. A small-caliber pistol was located on the floor near the body. Jewelry valued at more than $50,000 was untouched throughout the house.

A neighbor, J. W. Ashley, heard Dolly screaming for help. He went to the Oesterreichs' house to see if he could help, but when he opened the front door, he saw Fred lying in a pool of blood on the floor. He phoned the police who arrived minutes later.

Dolly told the investigators they returned home at 10:30 p.m. after spending the evening at a friend's house a few blocks away. Dolly said she headed upstairs to get ready for bed while Fred took care of a few things downstairs. She said as she approached the bedroom closet, someone suddenly appeared and shoved her inside the closet and locked the closet door from the outside. She recalled screaming for help while hearing a struggle downstairs and then four gunshots. Dolly said she then fell to the ground and went unconscious. Dolly told the investigators the burglars stole Fred's expensive watch.

During the coroner's inquest, another neighbor, Cora Norton, testified she did not believe she would have been able to hear Dolly screaming if indeed she had been locked in a closet. She explained, "they were too distant for that."

Dolly gave the coroner's jury a detailed description of what happened with details, including being shoved into the closet by burglars that were in their home when she and Fred returned from an evening out. Minutes later, she said, she heard a struggle and then gunshots downstairs.

Within hours, five men and one woman were arrested in connection with the murder. The six individuals were part of a criminal gang, and the police believed they were responsible for the murder. All six suspects were released after the police determined they were not involved.

Fred's attorneys in Milwaukee handled his estate. The Oesterreichs were well off due to Fred's apron manufacturing business. They had moved to Los Angeles from Milwaukee, Wisconsin, four years prior to the murder. Dolly received $142,000 from Fred's estate as well as the house they shared in Los Angeles. There was a stipulation in Fred's will stating that Dolly would inherit the house in Los Angeles if she was still living in the house one year after Fred's death.

The police continued to work on the case, and eleven months after the murder, Detective Lieutenant Herman Cline slapped a pair of handcuffs on Dolly and booked her into the county jail on a charge of murder in the first degree.

Earlier, J. E. Farber and Roy Klumb came forward and told the police that Dolly asked them to dispose of two .25-caliber pistols within days of the murder. She explained to them that although she was not involved in the murder, she did not want the police to find the guns in her house. The police were able to recover both of the firearms. One of the firearms was located at the edge of an oil pit on Wilshire Boulevard; the other was buried in a vacant lot.

Once Dolly was in police custody, they attempted to question her about the weapons. All she could say was, "I cannot say, I cannot say! I am too ill to answer … you will kill me if you question me further … I have done nothing for which I shall suffer … I will not answer … I am nearly insane…"

A friend of Dolly's, Attorney Herman Shapiro, who had done work for the Oesterreichs previously, visited Dolly in jail. He assured the waiting reporters that he would be able to prove Dolly's innocence in a court of law. Speaking to the throng of reporters, he stated: "My client will not say a word until I give her permission. I think it is more important this morning to tell about the rats that run over the cots in the woman's department of the city jail and make the women prisoners scream."

Herman went to see Detective Lieutenant Cline to discuss the case. Detective Lieutenant Cline immediately noticed Herman was wearing the watch Dolly claimed was stolen.

Later when Detective Lieutenant Cline questioned Dolly about the watch that he saw Herman wearing, she calmly stated: "Long after the murder I found the watch in the house. It had not been stolen because Fred was not wearing it that night. I gave it to Shapiro because he admired it."

At Dolly's first court appearance, Attorneys Frank Dominguez and H. L. Geisler represented her. She pled innocent to the charge of murder. Frank told reporters: "I am convinced of my client's innocence … I care nothing about the guns nor the conflicting statements or actions on the part of any hysterical woman. The thing that interests me keenly and will likewise interest a jury is how Mrs. Oesterreich got locked in that closet if she killed her husband…"[1]

From her jail cell, Dolly told the waiting reporters a bit about her past: "We never thought of ourselves as being well to do. We were never extravagant, but just lived well. Seven years ago our little boy, Raymond, died. My husband and I were terribly broken up over it, and he took up Christian Science."[2]

Dolly spoke of the apron manufacturing business:

> He had a factory here, but I sold it after he was killed because I really didn't want to run it without him. We had always worked together and the loneliness and everything made it just too hard for me to undertake it. I sold the business, and I sold our cars too. I was in such a nervous state that I couldn't drive, and I didn't enjoy the things Fred and I loved to do since he left.[3]

The trial was postponed numerous times. After serving more than one and a half years in jail, Dolly walked out a free woman. The District Attorney's Office was not certain they could obtain a guilty verdict and filed a motion to dismiss the case. All charges were dismissed, and Dolly was free to resume her life.

In a bizarre turn of events, a man by the name of Walter Klein (aka Otto Sanhuber) was arrested for murdering Fred. It had been eight years since the murder took place. It was Dolly's attorney friend, Herman Shapiro, who brought the case to Detective Lieutenant Cline and a team of detectives in April 1930.

Herman explained that when Dolly was in jail, she requested he go to her house and leave food out for her friend. She gave explicit instructions as to where to place the food and then said he needed to scratch on the wall and explained if he did so, "someone would appear."

Herman went onto say he did as Dolly requested, and a man came out of a hiding place in the attic. Herman said he continued to bring food to the man and over time they established a friendship. The team of detectives who listened to the story did a double take when Herman explained that Walter had been living in the Oesterreichs' attics for the past eighteen years as they moved from one house to another. He said Walter met Dolly when he did some repair work at Fred's factory in Milwaukee. Walter was twenty-one years old at the time. They began having an affair, and Dolly suggested he move into the attic of the house she shared with Fred.

Herman explained that when the Oesterreichs moved to Los Angeles, Walter followed and took up residence in the attic, just as he had done in Milwaukee. Herman said Fred never knew of Walter's presence. Dolly, he explained, would leave food for Walter when Fred was at home. Herman explained that when Fred was out of the house, Walter would come out of his hiding place.

Herman explained that one day when speaking with Walter, he confessed he was the one who shot Fred on August 22, 1922. Walter told him he heard Fred and Dolly arguing when they arrived home. He said he grabbed a gun and ran downstairs and shot Fred. He then locked Dolly in the closet and tossed the key on the floor of their bedroom.

Walter was indicted by the grand jury and later pled not guilty by reason of insanity at his arraignment. Dolly appeared before the grand jury. She, too, was indicted and pled not guilty at her arraignment.

Walter gave a statement to the anxious reporters who were covering this story around the world. Newspapers began referring to Walter as the "Bat Man." Walter explained: "Now that I've confessed, I feel a lot better. My conscious has always tormented me. The only thing I'm worried about now is how I'm going to explain this to my wife. I suppose I'll go to San Quentin, but I feel better and I'm glad it's over."

The investigation showed that Walter married Mathilda two years after the murder. By that time, Dolly was out of jail and was living alone in an apartment and she was no longer in touch with Walter.

Two months later, Walter's trial began in Superior Court Judge Carlos Hardy's courtroom. Deputy District Attorney James Costello represented the state of California. Earle Wakeman represented Walter.

The prosecution put Phillip Stover on the witness stand. Phillip was friends with Fred from Milwaukee. In speaking to the death of the Oesterreichs' child, Phillip said: "Mrs. Oesterreich did not seem at all affected by the death of the boy, although Fred was broken-hearted. The association between Mrs. Oesterreich and Otto [Walter] had begun before the child's death and continued afterward."[4]

Although Phillip never said that Fred knew that Walter was living in his attic, he did tell the jury that Fred knew that Walter and Dolly were involved as far back as when they lived in Milwaukee. He recalled Fred telling him that he asked Walter to leave Dolly alone.

A neighbor of the Oesterreichs testified that he had heard the couple arguing on several occasions. The jury heard from the two men who disposed of the firearms.

Herman testified about discovering that Walter had been staying in the Oesterreichs' attics for the past eighteen years. He described going to Dolly's house for the first time: "She told me to go to the room used as a storeroom and rap on the wall. I went to the room and whistled. An arm came out of the wall, a voice told me not to be afraid, and a man came through the closet wall." Herman identified Walter as the man who came out of the closet wall.

Walter took the witness stand and described the night of the murder for the jury. He explained his reason for living in the Oesterreichs' attics was "just to be near her." He admitted he had been living in attics wherever Dolly lived, both in Wisconsin and in California. Although Walter admitted to the police that he shot Fred after hearing Dolly and Fred arguing, he told the jury he shot Fred in self-defense, saying that Fred attacked him.

During his closing arguments, Deputy District Attorney Costello asked the jury to find Walter guilty and sentence him to death. Instead of murder, the jury found Walter guilty of manslaughter. The defense pointed out that the statute of limitations had run out for manslaughter and requested that Judge Hardy set aside the verdict. Judge Hardy agreed, and Walter walked out of jail a free man.

Dolly's trial began days after Walter was freed. The jury heard from Walter who admitted he had been living in the Oesterreichs' attic in order to be "close to Dolly." Walter explained to the jury that he shot Fred after hearing Dolly and Fred arguing in the downstairs portion of the house. Dolly took the witness stand and told the jury she witnessed Walter shoot her husband.

The jury of six men and six women were unable to reach a verdict after three days of deliberations. As the deliberations wore on, some voted for guilty of first-degree murder, others for second-degree murder. There were two jurors who held out for an acquittal. Judge Hardy discharged the jurors, and the prosecution began work on a new trial. Dolly was released on her own recognizance to await a new trial.

Two months after Dolly's first trial, the District Attorney's Office dismissed the case.

Six years after Fred was murdered, Dolly faced a $300,000 lawsuit brought by the wife of a man she had been involved with. Genevieve Hedrick claimed Dolly had alienated her husband, Ray, from her. Dolly filed an answer denying the charge. Ray in turn filed a cross-complaint stating Genevieve was "cruel and inhuman." A settlement was reached between Ray and Genevieve.

Thirty years later, Dolly married Ray. She died of cancer two weeks after the wedding. Dolly's estate was valued at more than $1 million at the time of her death in 1961. She left her entire estate to Ray. Ray told the media: "We have been in love for 30 years and we decided to marry because Dolly is terribly ill and must go to the hospital. As her husband, I will have the legal right to manage her estate which runs into millions of dollars' worth of property."

12
Charles Henry Schwartz

Residents of the quiet town of Walnut Creek were shaken by a huge explosion about 10 p.m. on the night of July 30, 1925. The explosion occurred at the Pacific Cellulose Company in Walnut Creek. The manufacturing business was managed by Charles Henry Schwartz who lived in Oakland with his wife, Alice, and their three boys, Clifford, Gordon, and Ralph.

Pacific Cellulose Company was created to manufacture artificial silk in a less expensive way than other procedures. The chemicals involved in the process were toxic for the firefighters who arrived to find the building completely engulfed. Inside the two-story building, firefighters located the body of a man in a closet. The body was badly burned and appeared to have died in the explosion.

Walter Gonzalez, who worked as the security guard at the manufacturing plant, told the police Charles sent him home "to take a nap for two hours" an hour before the explosion, which was highly unusual. Walter said he did leave the building, but minutes later he saw a blinding light followed by a roar and the explosion deafened the quiet night. He immediately grabbed a hose and applied water to the building.

Walter told the police he noticed that Charles had put a lock on the closet door two weeks before the explosion. He went onto say on the afternoon of the explosion, Charles became irate when he saw Walter's dog sniffing at the closet door. He said Charles kicked the dog away from the door.

Walter identified the body as that of Charles Schwartz. He explained that Charles had shown him he had exactly $1.73 in his pocket earlier in the day. The body had exactly $1.73 in the pants pocket. Walter recognized Charles' watch on his arm. He recalled Walter had borrowed a button for his collar earlier in the day. When he saw the body, he recognized the button he lent Charles.

The police contacted Alice who was distraught at the news that her husband died in the explosion. She told the police Charles phoned her five minutes before the explosion and said he was leaving the building and would be home soon. Alice identified the body as that of her husband by exclaiming, "That's him!

That's him!" She contacted their attorney, E. S. Bell, who also identified the body. With that, the case was closed as an accidental death.

Although Alice, her attorney, and Walter positively identified the burned body as that of Charles, not everyone was convinced. The adjuster for the life insurance company told the police the victim was 3 inches taller than Charles. Charles' physician, Dr. Reudy, examined the body twice, and was convinced the man was Charles. He discredited the insurance adjuster, saying that a person's height could change daily.

Criminologist Edward Oscar Heinrich of Berkeley was asked to examine the body. Criminologist Heinrich asked Alice what Charles had eaten for dinner on the night of the explosion. She said he had eaten cucumbers and beans. Neither of those food items were present in the stomach of the victim. He then asked Alice to provide some hair from Charles' hairbrush. When he examined the hairs from the hairbrush, they did not match the hair of the victim. He also noticed the watch that Walter recognized as Charles' turned out to be an inexpensive replica watch.

Criminologist Heinrich determined the man had been hit in the back of the head three times with a blunt object, causing his death. He went onto explain that the man was not alive when the explosion took place based on the fact the man's lungs did not have any smoke damage. The fingertips of the man had been cut off and acid had been poured on the hands in an effort to hinder identification of the body. Criminologist Heinrich also noted acid had been poured in the man's mouth in an effort to destroy the man's teeth.

After examining the Pacific Cellulose Company building, Criminologist Heinrich concluded that carbon disulphide had been spilled very methodically in a stream along the floor then ignited from the outside in a way that the flame would run to the closet where the body was located. Heinrich was able to trace the origin of the fire to the well of a bolt slot underneath the front door. Next to the slot he found a match that had been dropped into the liquid chemical that quickly caught fire, causing the explosion. Heinrich explained to Contra Costa Sheriff Veale that the hottest point of the fire was where the body lay, but it had not ignited beneath the body. He also noted that none of the chemical tubes or the windows had been broken, as they would have if an accident had caused the fire.

Heinrich further noted that although the manufacturing plant was set up to look like an impressive operation, the reality was that artificial silk had never been manufactured at the plant as Charles claimed.

Additional work was done on the body. Both Charles and the murder victim were missing the same tooth. However, when a dentist, Dr. Nielsen, examined the murder victim, he could tell the tooth had been yanked out and not surgically removed. In summary, he announced: "The dead man is not Schwartz. The teeth vary widely from Schwartz' teeth." Dr. Nielsen informed the police that Charles contacted him shortly before the explosion and inquired if molds of his teeth had been retained. He said Charles "seemed satisfied" when informed that the molds had been destroyed.

The police informed the media that the burned body was not Charles Schwartz, but instead was a victim of a homicide. They explained Charles faked his own death to collect a $180,000 insurance policy. In order to do so, he found a man of similar statue to himself and murdered him. After knocking out a tooth, planting $1.73 in his pocket, and placing an inexpensive replica watch on his wrist, he placed the body in a closet at the manufacturing plant.

Contra Costa Sheriff Veale further explained to the media: "The plot failed because the fire in the laboratory did not burn as long as [it] apparently was counted on. In another ten minutes the blaze would have so marked the body as to make identification other than Schwartz unlikely. There would have been no suspicion, no investigation and no exposition of another perfect crime."[1]

Contra Costa District Attorney A. B. Tinning told the press: "I am positive that the body is not that of Schwartz." When asked for further details, he explained: "If anything, he was too cunning. It was the evident attempt to destroy the possibility of identification that first aroused suspicion." At the end of the interview, District Attorney Tinning asked the reporters to announce that Charles was wanted for first-degree murder.

An arrest warrant was sworn out for Charles for first-degree murder. The wording of the arrest warrant read: "Leon Henry Schwartzhoff, alias Charles Henry Schwartz, alias John Doe Stein with the murder on or about July 30 of John Doe, a human being."

The police searched the Schwartz' home and discovered that all photographs of Charles were missing, as well as most of his clothing.

Charles' wife refused to believe her husband was capable of faking his own death, and steadfastly believed Charles perished in the explosion. She demanded that the body be turned over to her for burial. The police explained they would not be able to do so until the body was positively identified. She then offered to have the head decapitated so the police could continue their investigation and she could bury the rest of the body. The police quickly dismissed her request.

Discovering the identity of the deceased male proved to be a challenge. The police believed the body could be a man by the name of Joe Rodriguez. Joe had not been seen since the day of the explosion. The body was taken to the hospital and x-rayed to determine if the body had suffered any broken bones, which Joe had. As it turned out, Joe was found at a relative's house and was not aware he had been reported missing.

Criminologist Heinrich turned his attention to determining the identity of the victim. From the charred fragments of cloth, he determined that the man was wearing a denim shirt, overalls, and a hunting jacket at the time of his death.

He examined some scraps of burnt paper he had removed from the manufacturing plant. He put the burnt papers through a chemical process.

He could see that one page was a passage from St. John and other pages were religious tracts. He concluded the victim was a traveling missionary. He asked Sheriff Veale to run an article in local newspapers asking for the public's help in identifying the man.

Cecil Baker contacted Sheriff Veale and explained he believed the man was Gilbert Warren Barbe. He explained Gilbert was interested in chemistry and concluded he may have answered an ad Charles placed for an assistant.

A theory developed that Charles was abroad the freighter *Nordic* that was headed to Sweden. The freighter was searched at Westport, Oregon, but Charles was not on board.

Three women came forward and told the police they saw a man running from the Pacific Cellulose Company moments after the explosion. All three women lived near the manufacturing plant and rushed outside at the first sound of the explosion. One man told the police he saw a car speeding away from the manufacturing plant moments after the explosion.

The investigation revealed Elizabeth Adara had filed a $75,000 lawsuit against Charles for breach of promise weeks before the explosion. Elizabeth was from Switzerland, and in her lawsuit, she claimed Charles had promised to marry her. When she discovered Charles was married and using an alias, she filed the lawsuit. In response, Charles stated Elizabeth was part of a group of chemists who were trying to steal his formula for manufacturing artificial silk. Days before the explosion, he gave a deposition wherein he admitted he gave Elizabeth a diamond ring but denied he ever promised to marry her.

Captain Clarence Lee of the Berkeley Police Department came forward with information regarding Charles' keen interest in "perfect crimes." He said Charles would visit the police station and spend hours asking questions about how law enforcement solved murders. Captain Lee explained:

> Schwartz seemed particularly interested in the failure of criminals to hide traces of their crime. He also professed special interest in American police methods for catching criminals and tracing missing persons. He tried to give the impression that he worked as a detective in Europe, but when I asked him about his experiences, he was always vague in his answers.[2]

A bank manager in Oakland saw Alice at a safe deposit box four days after the explosion and phoned the police. Alice left the bank before the police arrived, but they learned the Schwartz' had rented a safe deposit box using an alias. Further investigation revealed Charles had been using the alias H. Orchard and A. E. Orchard. Alice had been using the alias Alice E. Orchard and Alice E. Warden. The Schwartz' attorney, E. S. Bell, told reporters that the assumed names were due to Alice using her maiden name of Orchard and her previous married name of Warden.

An office worker told the police Charles asked her to purchase $8.50 worth of silk material at a local store that he passed off as his own work.

The public continued to call in information to the police. An automobile salesperson said Charles purchased a new car days before the explosion, explaining he needed the car to get to the Mojave Desert. A mechanic told law enforcement Charles purchased two new tires the day before the explosion, and explained he planned to drive to Portland, Oregon.

Law enforcement chased one tip after another, but nothing panned out until N. B. Edmonds of Oakland picked up a newspaper and saw a photograph of Charles with a caption of "Wanted for Murder." Edmonds and his wife thought the photograph looked like their new neighbor, Harold Warren. Edmonds immediately phoned the police and spoke with Captain Clarence Lee.

The police rushed to an apartment in Oakland. The apartment manager directed them to a room on the second floor. The police bounded up the stairs, quickly found the correct apartment, and began shouting, "Police Open Up." They barely had the words out when a shot rang out. They forced their way into the apartment and found Charles dead from a gunshot wound to the head. They discovered a letter Charles had written to Alice. In the note, he claimed he killed Gilbert in self-defense after Gilbert attacked him when he refused to hire him or give him money. Charles signed the letter, "I kiss this in bidding and kissing you goodbye. My last kiss is for you Alice."

13

San Diego Murders

When Virginia Brooks, age ten, did not arrive at school on February 11, 1931, her parents contacted the local police and sheriff deputies in Euclid and in San Diego. Law enforcement asked local citizens to assist them in searching for the young girl. They searched more than 15 square miles of brush-covered hills, every vacant house, and every culvert but came up empty handed. Soon after, San Diego Chief of Police Arthur Hill asked 200 Boy Scouts to join in the search.

Fearing that Virginia had been kidnapped and murdered, the police sent telegrams to all cities in California. One law enforcement officer told reporters: "We are doing everything we can, but we don't know which way to turn."

Virginia's parents were just as perplexed as the police. They had recently moved from Portland, Oregon, with Virginia and her two brothers, Gordon and George. Prior to that, the family lived in Indianapolis, Indiana. They told reporters: "We have no enemies. I can't understand why anyone should take our child."

Virginia's aunt, Lilly Campbell, traveled from Los Angeles to be of assistance. She provided a photograph that law enforcement used in mailing out flyers throughout California.

Those who had lived in San Diego for a period of time recalled the unsolved murder of Nicholas Esparza, age eleven, in 1927. Nicholas' remains were found months after he was last seen alive at Camp Kearney Mesa. Although one suspect confessed to murdering a young boy, the police were never able to determine if Nicholas was the victim of that particular murder.

An anonymous resident of San Diego offered a $500 reward for the arrest and conviction of the person(s) responsible for kidnapping Virginia.

The public provided tips, including one woman who believed she saw Virginia walking next to a man on the day she disappeared. Two other people thought they saw Virginia in a car with a man the afternoon she was last seen. A few men were brought in for questioning but were released soon after. One tipster told the police he saw a girl resembling the photograph of Virginia with a man in a car that had Kansas license plates.

A tip was called in from someone saying they saw a girl resembling Virginia near the edge of a lake in San Diego. Based on that information, sheriff deputies dragged the lake, but came up empty handed. They located footprints near the lake that they believed were a match to Virginia's shoes.

The military joined in the search. They dispatched airplanes to fly low over the hills and canyons surrounding areas of San Diego. As the days passed, news of Virginia's disappearance spread across the country. The deputies in San Diego found themselves inundated with possible sightings of Virginia all across the country. None of the tips panned out, and they remained stumped as to what happened to the child.

As the search continued, law enforcement expanded their search into Mexico and Arizona. There had been four sightings of a girl resembling Virginia with a man in Arizona. Sheriff deputies traveled to Arizona to conduct a search, but nothing was found, and they returned home.

Two weeks later, Virginia's father, John Brooks, traveled to Quartzsite, Arizona. The police in San Diego received a letter stating a man was holding Virginia captive in a secluded cabin in Quartzsite. Once in Arizona, John met up with Yuma County sheriff deputies who accompanied him to Quartzsite and performed a thorough search. The search did not turn up any evidence, and John returned home.

Twenty-seven days after Virginia left for school, her body was found in an isolated section of Camp Kearney Mesa by sheep herder, George Moses. Her head had been decapitated, but her torso, arms, and legs were intact. George informed Deputy Sheriff Blake Mason the burlap bag the body was in was not at the location the day before. The grass underneath the burlap bag was still green, leading law enforcement to believe Virginia was killed somewhere else and placed in the isolated area.

Detectives took a plaster cast of a tire track near the body. They also discovered two blonde hairs on Virginia's hand. There was a rubber glove nearby and a scrap of newspaper. Virgina's schoolbooks were located near the burlap bag. The spot where the body was located was 10 miles from the Brooks' house.

Virginia's mother clasped a Valentine Virginia had made days before she was murdered. Through her sobs, she cried: "Why should it have been our little girl? It cannot be true, I'll try to bear it, but I am afraid I cannot stand it." Virginia's father said: "I'd tear his throat out with my bare hands if I could catch the man who did this."

Within hours of the discovery of Virginia's body, the police arrested a man who lived near the Brooks' house and who witnesses said they saw driving a car with Virginia as the passenger. He was released after the detectives confirmed his alibi and no charges were filed. Two other men were held for questioning, but they were released soon after. Detectives and sheriff deputies kept six men under surveillance, but they were unable to build a case against any of them.

After examining the body, the coroner issued a statement saying Virginia was murdered within a day of being kidnapped. Neither Dr. F. E. Toomey, county autopsy surgeon, or Dr. Ernst Mundkowski, county hospital chemist, were able to determine the cause of death, but they were able to say the skull had not been fractured.

A service was held for Virginia at Roger's Chapel. The crowd overflowed into the streets with traffic backed up for miles. Undercover police attended the service to scan the crowds for anything suspicious, but no leads were developed.

Lieutenant Wyman Ward questioned a man who lived 3 miles from where Virginia's body was discovered. The police believed the tire tracks of his car matched the plaster cast they made near Camp Kearney Mesa. The man admitted he worked in a hospital, so the police believed he could have obtained a rubber glove such as the one found near the body. The man was not arrested, and the police resumed their investigation.

Governor James Rolph sent Harry Hickok and M. F. Muemburg, with the State Bureau of Investigation, to assist with the investigation. They worked on identifying the tire tracks which they believed were from a retread, not an original tread. They also worked on identifying the two hairs found on Virginia's hand. They searched all barns and outbuildings in the vicinity of Camp Kearney Mesa and studied the dirt and leaves near where the body was located.

The Brooks requested that the investigators interview a young man who lived near them. Virginia's mother told reporters: "We cannot make a direct accusation against this young man, but we will feel relieved if you can assure us that he had no hand in this terrible thing." The man was questioned, but he was not charged with the crime.

The Brooks received three death threats. The first two letters were slipped under the front door of their house; the other was sent through the mail.

Governor Rolph offered a $10,000 reward for the arrest and conviction of the person(s) responsible for Virginia's murder. Despite running down more than 500 tips and interviewing 300 people, the police and sheriff deputies were stumped. As they continued to work on the case, another case demanded their attention.

Eight days after Virginia's body was found, sheriff deputies in San Diego were called to Black Mountain for a body hanging from an oak tree. The female was nude and had been strangled and hit on the head. It appeared the victim had fought off her attackers based on having skin underneath her fingernails. The victim's clothes were neatly folded near the oak tree.

The police investigation revealed the female was seventeen-year-old Louise Teuber. Louise attended high school and worked at a local 5 and 10 cent store. She lived with her father, William, and her grandmother. Her older sister, Isabel, was married and lived nearby.

One detail the detectives noticed was that the knot on the rope had been tied by someone who was familiar with a sailor's knot. A friend of Louise's told the deputies Louise had been dating a sailor. Detectives interviewed several men who were acquaintances of Louise's, but no arrests were made.

Sheriff Ed Cooper received information that Louise was with two young men and a young woman prior to her death.

The coroner determined Louise was alive, but probably unconscious, when she was hanged from the tree. The coroner's examination revealed Louise had been struck behind her right ear, causing her to lose consciousness. The coroner believed Louise was lying on the ground when the rope was placed around her neck.

Louise's father answered the media's questions after rumors began to swirl that Louise had run away from home. He stated he spent long hours working as a barber while his mother helped with the children: "We did the best we could." He said he admonished her for sneaking out two nights before she was murdered.

Louise's father turned over a letter he received the day after her body was discovered. The letter was postmarked hours before she was killed. In the letter, she told her father she was not returning home. Louise's sister also received a letter. Both letters were postmarked at the same time. The letter to her sister read, in part, "I am going as far away as I can. Maybe I'm dippy, but try and forget me." In closing, Louise asked her sister not to worry about her. The detectives were not certain if Louise had written the letters of her own free will or if the murderer forced her to. They believed by Louise saying she was leaving, no one would report her missing.

Detectives searched Louise's bedroom. They read her diary, but there were no entries for the week prior to her murder. Within the pages of her diary, she used initials when writing about her boyfriend. The detectives interviewed her friends and learned she was dating a young man who served in the military. They detained several men who were stationed nearby, but no arrests were made. Several other men were detained but no charges were filed.

Sheriff Cooper requested the assistance of the sheriff at Fort Morgan, Colorado, in questioning a man he believed was the murderer. The man said he was in Nebraska at the time of the murder. His alibi checked out, and he was not charged with the murder.

The investigators were not making any progress on either Virginia or Louise's murder when they were notified of yet another murder in San Diego. "Diamond Dolly" Bibbens, age thirty-four, was found strangled to death in her apartment a month after Louise was murdered. Her apartment had been ransacked and her diamonds were missing.

The detectives could tell that Dolly put up a fight with her attacker based on having skin underneath her fingernails. Police Captain P. Hayes immediately told reporters: "The killer is an underworld character, and the motive was underworld revenge." He would not give any further details.

The autopsy showed Dolly had been strangled with a towel. Additionally, she had been stabbed seventeen times in the head and abdomen.

The police believed they knew who was responsible for the murder of Dolly. Henry Yardley, a friend of Dolly's, had not been seen since the night she was murdered. The investigation revealed Henry pawned a purse belonging to Dolly in St. Joseph, Montana, days after the murder.

San Diego Detective William Lloyd traveled to Pennsylvania to arrest Henry Yardley. He was returned to California and held without bail. He admitted he had been friends with Dolly but said she gave him the purse to pawn. At the preliminary hearing, it was determined there was not enough evidence against Henry to continue the case. Henry claimed he left San Diego days prior to the murder, and the prosecution was not able to prove otherwise. He walked out of the courtroom a free man.

Just when law enforcement had their hands full with three homicides, they were called to yet another homicide. Hazel Bradshaw, age twenty-three, was murdered in Balboa Park, just outside of San Diego's business district.

Hazel had worked as a telephone operator for the past three years. She lived with her parents, two younger sisters, and a younger brother. Hazel was engaged to W. S. Wilson, age twenty-four. He told the investigators a man by the name of Moss E. Garrison threatened to kill Hazel and himself a week before Hazel was murdered. One of Hazel's younger sisters also informed the police that Moss frequently threatened to murder Hazel.

The police arrested Moss who denied murdering Hazel; instead, he claimed he took her home Saturday night and heard her close the door to her house. The police noticed he had a bandage on his finger which they believed was from the struggle that took place before the murder. Once Moss was booked into the jail, he requested to see Hazel's body.

Several detectives accompanied Moss to the mortuary where he was permitted to view Hazel's body. He appeared nonplussed when he saw the seventeen stab wounds. He touched her hair and kissed her forehead while mumbling, "My little sweetheart." As they prepared to leave the mortuary, Moss kissed Hazel's forehead one last time.

The case went to trial two months after the murder. Moss took the witness stand and adamantly denied murdering Hazel. He said he told a police officer he loved Hazel and did not kill her. He then told the jurors: "Then I told him about the automobile I had seen parked near her house at that time, and that she told me two days before that a sailor boy had threatened her. I told them that if they would find out who was in the car and investigate the threat that they would know who murdered Hazel."[1]

Under cross examination, the prosecution asked Moss who he believed killed Hazel. He replied, "From my best information I have concluded that two men did it. I don't know their names, but I think one of them was called, 'Harry.'" He went onto explain that one of Hazel's coworkers overheard her say it was all over with Harry.

The prosecution called Julia Stone to the witness stand. She testified she was driving the automobile Moss mentioned. A sailor testified to seeing Moss the day before the murder and noticing he had a bandaged finger. A woman who lived near the park where Hazel was murdered testified that she did not hear any screams that night. One man testified to being with Moss when he learned Hazel had been killed. He told the jurors Moss was startled at the news.

The defense contended "gangsters killed Hazel Bradshaw." Defense attorney Abijah Fairchild emphasized that the police were under pressure to make an arrest after four females were murdered in that many months.

The jury panel that was made up of nine men and three women. They deliberated for two hours before returning a verdict of not guilty.

Three years passed, and then sixteen-year-old Celia Cota was found murdered in her backyard. Celia left the home she shared with her parents and younger sister, about 8 p.m. on August 18, 1934, to go for a short walk. When she failed to return home, her parents contacted the San Diego Police Department. The police located Celia's badly beaten body in the family's backyard.

The police questioned Celia's boyfriend but soon cleared him after he provided an alibi. One man who had been arrested in El Paso, Texas, came under suspicion when he told his fellow inmates he knew Celia. When detectives with the San Diego Police Department interviewed him in Texas, he was able to prove he was in New Mexico when Celia was murdered.

Lester Beard was arrested on suspicion of murder. Sheriff Keate and three extra jail guards kept constant vigil after they learned some of the inmates planned to attack Lester. When interviewed by detectives, Lester denied having anything to do with the crime, even saying he had never heard of Celia prior to being arrested. Lester was released as a suspect after the detectives interviewed him.

Two other men were questioned before being released after it was determined they were not involved. Another man was arrested in Los Angeles and held in the city jail until detectives from San Diego could interview him. The detectives determined he was not involved. Days later, they made another arrest but soon released the suspect.

As the weeks and months went by, other arrests and interviews took place, but no one was ever charged with Celia's murder.

Five years after Virginia was murdered, another female was raped and murdered. Ruth Muir, age thirty-five, was found in a cove along the beach in La Jolla on August 31, 1936. Ruth had worked as a secretary at the Y.W.C.A. in Riverside for seven years. She was visiting La Jolla with her parents who lived in Texas. Her parents reported Ruth missing when she did not return to their rental cottage after going outside to move her car.

The detectives found a piece of concrete with what they believed were bloodstains 40 feet from Ruth's body. The piece of concrete was approximately 6 inches wide and 8 inches long. Detective Meade told reporters: "It was just about as far away as a man could throw it. It was shaped so that it had a sort of handle which would have made it easy to grasp. We can't tell until a thorough examination if it actually is the weapon used." The police took apart a nearby storm drain to look for evidence. They also examined some loose hairs that Ruth was clutching in her hand. There was no beneficial evidence from any of these items.

Ten detectives searched every inch of the cove where Ruth's body was located. Four divers took to the ocean near the cove in the hopes of locating evidence, but nothing came of either search.

Seven men were questioned but released soon afterwards. A witness provided a description of a man seen near where Ruth's body was found. The police sent teletypes to nearby states with a description of the suspect. The city council, the mayor, and a resident each offered a $500 reward for the arrest and conviction for the person(s) responsible.

As the police continued to chase down leads, Ruth was laid to rest in San Antonio, Texas, where her parents lived.

Three weeks after the murder, Donald Hazell confessed to killing Ruth. The police first contacted him days after the murder. At that time, he was mumbling incoherently about the murder. His family provided an alibi for the night the murder took place. His confession was disregarded after the superintendent of a local psychiatric hospital told law enforcement that Donald "would confess anything."

Harry Hickok, of the State Bureau of Criminal Identification, was put in charge of the murder case. He told reporters:

> Our investigation at Riverside has convinced us that Miss Muir had no enemies in Riverside who might plot her death.
>
> Personally, I have seldom seen a woman who was universally loved and respected as Miss Muir was among her Riverside friends. Her life was spotless and her reputation an example for all.
>
> It is my personal opinion that a sadistic degenerate committed this slaying and our investigation here narrows our probe to the San Diego area.[2]

Another man confessed to murdering Ruth, but his confession was determined to be invalid. As the year closed out, more men were detained and questioned, but no arrests were made. The year 1937 brought more interviews, but no arrests, and the case joined the others in the cold case file.

"I'm tired of living. You got to do me a favor. You get me the gas chamber," were the words Wilbert Felix Friend spoke on May 30, 1955 to newspaper reporter, Mark Waters, with the *San Diego Union*. Wilbert phoned Mark from a hotel in San Juan Capistrano. Mark asked Wilbert several questions before notifying San Diego Police Lieutenant Mort Geer.

Lieutenant Geer and San Diego Police Sergeant Paul Walk left immediately for San Juan Capistrano. While they were enroute to San Juan Capistrano, Wilbert made a second collect call to Mark. He quickly stated: "I want to see you tonight. Come up here yourself and get me."

Lieutenant Geer and Sergeant Walk contacted Wilbert who repeated his confession and was able to recall details of the murder that took place nineteen years ago. Wilbert emphasized: "I'm tired of running ... I'm sick of remorse."

The one thing that always bothered the detectives was not being able to determine what the murder weapon was. Wilbert explained he used a "green club," explaining that it was a piece of wood from a bench. Wilbert offered up the motive, saying it was robbery, although it turned out that Ruth's purse was empty.

Once Wilbert was booked into jail on suspicion of murder, Lieutenant Geer did additional research and learned that Wilbert worked as a golf caddy at a club in La Jolla at the time of the murder. Wilbert had been questioned at the time but released for lack of evidence. Wilbert had been arrested previously for sex offenses. At the time of Wilbert's arrest, he was on probation for a rape conviction.

The police were not convinced of Wilbert's confession, having been through other false confessions. They gave Wilbert a lie detector test, and it indicated he was telling the truth about the murder. Lieutenant Geer told reporters: "It could well be he is telling the truth."

The detective team took Wilbert back to the scene of the crime and asked him to reenact what transpired at the cove nineteen years ago. He explained he was living in a tent on the beach at the time of the murder. He noticed Ruth sitting on a bench in the moonlight and he forced her into the cove, raped her, and bludgeoned her to death.

Wilbert pled innocent and innocent by reason of insanity, but later withdrew that plea. The trial began three months after Wilbert confessed. Superior Court Judge John Hewicker presided over the proceedings. The jury consisted of seven women and five men.

Many of the police who worked on the investigation testified about the investigation. A recording of Wilbert's confession was played for the jury. Sergeant Walk testified to the extent the police went to ensure Wilbert's confession was legitimate. Mark explained to the jury how he received two collect calls from Wilbert confessing to murdering Ruth. After a two-day trial, the jury began deliberating at 3 p.m. They deliberated until 1 a.m. before retiring for the night. They began deliberating again at 9 a.m. Soon after, they announced their verdict: guilty of murder in the first-degree. The verdict brought a mandatory death penalty.

Wilbert later told the media: "If I had it to do all over again, I don't think I would have confessed. It caused too much fuss for my friends and relatives." He also said he kept quiet for nineteen years so as to not cause his relatives any grief.

Days later, Judge Hewicker formally sentenced Wilbert to die in the gas chamber at San Quentin prison.

The State Supreme Court upheld the verdict but ruled that a new trial would need to be held to determine if life imprisonment or death was in order. They believed the prosecutor erred in arguing that there were no mitigating circumstances. They ruled: "The statute no more suggests that punishment be death in the absence of mitigating circumstances than it suggests the penalty be life imprisonment in the absence of aggravating circumstances." They added: "… a jury is entitled to weigh a case and reach a verdict without any advice from the district attorney."

A new trial was held, and the jury recommended the death penalty. Hearing this for the second time, Wilbert bolted for the courtroom door. Two deputies caught up to him and the three of them fell to the ground. The deputies were able to subdue Wilbert and he was returned to the defendant's table. Wilbert began a hunger strike once he was back at San Quentin prison.

The State Supreme Court upheld the verdict with a vote of 4–3 and a date was set for the execution. A few months later, Governor Goodwin Knight asked the State Supreme Court to lessen the penalty. The State Supreme Court recommended clemency. Governor Knight commuted the sentence to life imprisonment two days before Wilbert was to be executed. Wilbert was forty-eight years when he began his life sentence in 1959.

On January 15, 1947, the body of a female was found in a vacant lot in San Diego. The body had been badly mutilated, raped, and cut in half at the waist. The female was identified as Elizabeth Short, age twenty-two, based on her fingerprints that were on file from a federal job application.

An autopsy revealed Elizabeth died from shock, hemorrhaging, and a concussion. The autopsy physicians determined the killer had used a knife to cut Elizabeth's face 3 inches on each side of her mouth while she was still alive. Elizabeth had suffered a concussion from repeated blows to her head. The killer had mutilated her body after she died.

Elizabeth's mother, Phoebe Short, flew from Medford, Massachusetts, to San Diego. Elizabeth's sister and brother-in-law traveled from Berkeley to assist with the investigation. Elizabeth's father who resided in California informed the detectives he had not been in touch with Elizabeth for three years. Elizabeth was laid to rest on a foggy day in Oakland with only her relatives present.

The detectives were able to determine Elizabeth worked as a clerk for the U.S. Army during World War II at Camp Cooke in Santa Barbara County. She was an aspiring actress who was known by the nickname "Black Dahlia," due to her jet-black hair and her penchant for wearing black clothing.

Witnesses came forward and reported Elizabeth had been seen with a young man who went by the name of "Red." San Diego Chief of Police C. B. Horrall put out an all-points bulletin with a description of "Red" and the automobile they believed he was driving.

Within days, the police arrested Robert Manley who they believed was responsible for murdering Elizabeth. Robert denied any involvement in the murder and claimed he had not seen Elizabeth for two weeks. He agreed to take a lie detector test, but the test was inconclusive after he continually drifted off to sleep despite the detectives plying him with coffee. A chemical analysis of Robert's automobile failed to turn up any bloodstains. Robert told the detectives that two weeks before Elizabeth's murder, he noticed large scratches on her arms. She attributed the injuries to an "intensely jealous" boyfriend. He described the boyfriend as being of Italian descent who lived in San Diego. Robert was released from custody.

Two weeks after Elizabeth's body was found, postal employees saw a thick envelope addressed to "*Los Angeles Examiner* and other newspapers." The employees contacted the San Diego Police Department and detectives took possession of the envelope. The sender had cut words out of newspapers and glued them to the envelope instead of handwriting the address. Inside the envelope, the police located Elizabeth's birth certificate and social security card, her address book, six photographs, and personal papers, some of which were dated days before she was murdered. At the bottom of the envelope, in cut-out words, it said "Here is Dahlia's belongings. Letter to follow." The envelope had a strong scent of gasoline, leading the detectives to believe the sender attempted to destroy any fingerprints. Nevertheless, they were able to lift fingerprints and send them to Washington, D.C., for comparison to all fingerprints on file. The fingerprints failed to identify a suspect. The detectives interviewed the people identified in Elizabeth's address book, but they were not able to identify any suspects.

Days later, the *Los Angeles Examiner* received a postcard with the words "Here it is. Turning in Wednesday, January 29th, 10 a.m. Had my fun at police." The postcard was signed "Black Dahlia Avenger."

The morning of January 29, another note was sent with the words "Changed mind. Find me." This was followed by a note that read: "Five tomorrow evening at the *Los Angeles Times*. Promise. Black Dahlia. B.B." The next note read: "Have changed my mind. You would not give me a square deal. Dahlia killing was justified." The last note said he would surrender if he received no more than ten years. Cut out newspaper words were used to convey each message. The police issued a statement:

> Assuming that these messages are authentic and have been sent by the killer, such persons should know that it is not within the power of any police officer or any police department to make terms, and the sentence upon conviction for such acts lies within the discretion of the courts.
>
> However, all police officers are well aware that there are two sides to every story, and we can only promise that you will receive fair treatment and a just trial.[3]

The police did not receive any more letters.

Law enforcement in Breckenridge, Colorado, detained Fred Woodley, as a material witness because they believed he knew who killed Elizabeth. Fred admitted he and a female friend spent time with Elizabeth and her male companion the night before she was murdered. He recalled Elizabeth introduced the man as "Jack." Fred described the male as having red hair and wearing a U.S. Navy chief petty officer uniform. He said the male companion was intoxicated and belligerent. He did mention that the man had a tattoo with the initials "J.W." on his right hand and was missing a finger on that hand.

Fred went onto say they parted company and he returned to his hotel room:

Later that night, the sailor called at my hotel and said he was in a jam. He told he had been in an accident. His clothes were bloody. He asked if he could borrow one of my suits. I lent him one and kept the soiled clothes.

He came back next morning and we poked the bloody clothing down a sewer some distance from my hotel. I do not recall clearly just where all this happened. I had been on a pretty good bender myself. I do know, though, that Jack and the Dahlia had been keeping company off and on for some time before I met them.[4]

Fred was released after the police were unable to locate the suspect he described.

The police questioned U.S. Army Corporal Joseph Dumais at length, after he confessed to killing Elizabeth. Joseph signed a fifty-page confession, but many of the details did not match up. He admitted he had been on a date with Elizabeth a week before the body was discovered, however, he also said he had blacked out and could not remember anything of that night. Joseph was cleared of all suspicion after his military records showed he was at a military base in New Jersey when Elizabeth was murdered.

By the one-year anniversary of the discovery of Elizabeth's body, fifty-nine suspects had been cleared of any wrongdoing. Eleven subjects had confessed to murdering Elizabeth, but the police determined they were not involved. Tips continued to pour into the police headquarters, but nothing ever panned out. The case remains unsolved to this day.

14

Juanita "The Duchess" Spinelli

"Bea I'm shot—shot in the stomach" were the last words spoken by Leland Cash on April 8, 1940 before he succumbed to his injuries. The police arrived at the barbeque stand at Lincoln Way and La Playa Streets in San Francisco where Leland and his wife, Beatrice, worked. They discovered Leland deceased near the back door of the restaurant.

San Francisco Police Lieutenant Michael Mitchell and Inspectors George Engler, Harry Husted, and Al Corrasa concluded it was a simple robbery. They learned Leland was hard of hearing and may not have been able to understand what the robber was saying and was shot during the chaos.

Beatrice explained to the police they usually took food home at midnight when they closed the barbeque stand. She said Leland was carrying food out to their car, and she was cleaning the kitchen, when she heard a loud noise and then heard her husband calling for her. The police believed the robber mistook the food packages for the bank bag.

The police closed the case as a robbery. That was until the California Highway Patrol received a phone call from Albert Ives, age twenty-one. Albert told the California Highway Patrol he was traveling with four other people, and when they stopped to get a beverage, he snuck away to make a phone call.

Albert went on to say that the female in the car was Juanita Spinelli, age fifty, who called herself the "The Duchess." According to Albert, Juanita operated a gang that was responsible for murdering Leland as well as murdering a member of her own gang. Albert explained days after she ordered the murder of Leland, she decided to murder Robert Sherrard, age eighteen, for fear he would tell someone about the murder of Leland. Albert provided the California Highway Patrol with a description of the car and the license plate they were traveling in.

The California Highway Patrol conducted a traffic stop near Truckee and took Juanita, her common-law husband, Mike Simeone, age thirty-two, Gordon Hawkins, age thirty-two, and Albert into custody. Juanita's daughter, Lorraine "Gypsy" Spinelli, age nineteen, was detained as a material witness.

Investigators interviewed each of the suspects. They each admitted their part in the murders of Leland and Robert.

The investigators interviewed Albert at length. He said Juanita gave him the gun and he admitted he was the one who fired the weapon that killed Leland. He said they left without any money after everything went wrong at the barbeque stand. Albert did not have an explanation as to why Juanita ordered the murder of Leland.

Albert further stated they held up a gas station later that night and received $22. Albert explained they were driving a stolen car during both hold ups. Albert said Juanita had threatened to "bump him off," and after seeing what she ordered for Robert, he began to fear for his own life and decided to place a phone call to the California Highway Patrol.

Albert went into more details about the murder of Robert. He recalled the four of them went on a picnic along the Sacramento River. During the picnic they plotted ways in which to kill Robert. The suggestions included tying him to a railroad track, running him over with a car, shooting him in the back, or drowning him. The group decided to go with the later because Juanita wanted him to have a "merciful death." Albert said Juanita put some "knockout drops" in the whiskey Robert was drinking. Albert went onto explain that once Robert passed out, Juanita hit him over the head. Albert and Gordon then drove Robert to a bridge over the Sacramento River and tossed him into the water. Albert said when he placed the telephone call, the group was on their way to Texas where they planned to pull one last "big job" before heading to Mexico.

Juanita told the detectives she planned to return to Detroit and have Albert arrested. She placed the blame for Robert's murder squarely on Albert. Juanita admitted to being aware of Robert's murder but quickly added she "wanted it to be a mercy killing, because I kind of liked the boy."

After hours of interviews, the detectives were able to ascertain that Albert, Robert, and Gordon were present when Leland was murdered. They determined that Mike was responsible for finding places for the gang to rob, and Lorraine was responsible for luring male robbery victims. Their investigation revealed that Gordon, who was skilled in auto mechanics, was the one who stole the vehicles they used for their crimes. District Attorney J. Francis O'Shea filed first-degree murder charges against Juanita, Mike, Gordon, and Albert.

District Attorney Otis Babcock told the media he was going to seek the death penalty against Juanita, emphasizing that she would be the first woman to be executed in California's gas chamber.

Juanita, Gordon, and Albert pled not guilty and not guilty by reason of insanity for the murder of Robert. Mike pled not guilty. The trial began one month after the arrests and indictments.

Both Juanita and Mike told the jury that Albert was responsible for Robert's murder. Mike emphasized, "Ives wanted to get rid of Bob because he talked too much." The prosecution questioned why Juanita did not go to the authorities after Robert was killed. She replied: "I was afraid to go to the police—I've told you that dozens of times. I was afraid of what Al said would happen to my daughter. He was going to put her in a Chinese hop joint so she would be 'rotten' in six months. Yes, I was afraid."[1]

Albert took the witness stand and quietly admitted he threw Robert into the Sacramento River but quickly added: "I got my orders to get rid of Sherrard. They were talking about some way of getting rid of me, afterwards, when we were driving up toward Reno. They talked about a 700-foot cliff—that's a nice drop."[2]

Albert was asked how he came to know Juanita. He said he grew up in an orphanage, and when he first met Juanita, he was "treated like one of the family." He went on to say: "Then, there was a bunch of guys in the duchess' house one time and they were talking about the purple gang, and 'jobs' and that stuff. They showed me two blackjacks and a gun and said I'd be hung if I talked. I never left the gang alone after that. There'd always be another guy with me."[3]

Before Albert stepped down from the witness stand, he told the jury that Mike gave Robert the whiskey with the drugs in it and proceeded to beat Robert into unconsciousness. According to Albert, Juanita also participated in beating Robert. Albert admitted he followed Mike's orders and removed Robert's clothes and put swimming trunks on him before throwing him in the Sacramento River. He explained the reason for putting swimming trunks on Robert was to make it appear that he drowned.

From the witness stand, Juanita was quick to state, "I never laid a hand on the man." She did, however, admit that she provided what she called "knockout crystals."

Mike told the jury that he did not know that Juanita had drugged Robert, but he did admit he gave Robert several drinks of whiskey during their picnic. Gordon admitted he was the one who drove the car to the Sacramento River.

The jury quickly found Juanita, Mike, Gordon, and Albert guilty of first-degree murder. The jury did not recommend leniency, meaning they would be executed.

Juanita's daughter, Lorraine, was initially held as a material witness, but she was released after the trial. Weeks later, when Juanita was housed at the Tehachapi Prison, she wrote a letter to the detectives in Sacramento. The letter read, in part: "I wish to make a complete confession that my daughter, Lorraine Spinelli, is equally guilty as I was in the knowledge of the Robert Sheppard [Sherrard] death and I am asking you to take her into custody and that she be tried for same."[4]

Juanita advised that Lorraine was hitchhiking to Reno, adding, "for the same purpose as she was doing in 'Frisco. This only means more thefts and maybe more lives, so please stop her."

The investigators did not arrest Lorraine, as they did not believe she participated in the murder, or even had knowledge of it. Juanita's two younger sons, ages eleven and sixteen, were placed in an orphanage after she was arrested.

Albert was sentenced to the Mendocino State Hospital for the Insane instead of being executed. After two reprieves, the day came that Juanita became the first female to be executed in California's gas chamber. Juanita confessed to a priest before eating her final meal consisting of bacon, toast, and black coffee. She taped photographs of her three children across her heart on her green dress before she was led into the gas chamber. At 10:25 a.m. on November 21, 1941, Juanita took her final breath.

A week later, Mike and Gordon were led to the gas chamber after finishing their final meal of bacon and eggs, potatoes, toast, fruit, and coffee. They died in the same room, at the same time.

15
Escape from Alcatraz

For as long as there were prisoners held at Alcatraz prison, there were plans hatched by inmates to make a great escape. Beginning in the 1850s, the U.S. Army used Alcatraz as a military prison. During the Civil War and the Spanish-American War, the U.S. government held prisoners on the foreboding rock.

There were many early day escapes including one in 1862 when three prisoners used a file to remove their leg chains. They used a rope to lower themselves down to the water and stole a boat and made a clean getaway.

A few years later, nine prisoners broke the lock off a boathouse and stole a boat with the assistance of a guard. The prisoners made it to San Francisco where a few of them were arrested, but others were never located.

In 1890, two inmates made their way down to the water and climbed into a skiff. They made it to the shore with guards close behind, but they managed to escape.

Jesse Adams was sent to Alcatraz in 1900 after being convicted of murdering a fellow member of the military while they were serving in the Philippines. After being at Alcatraz for a short time, Jesse stowed away in a 3-foot by 2-foot box. The box was shipped from Alcatraz to the Presidio Wharf where Jesse walked away. He was arrested four days later in Sacramento.

In 1902, Tom Wilmore was serving in the Phillippines when a card game went drastically wrong and Tom began firing his gun, which resulted in the murder of two fellow military personnel. Two other military personnel were wounded. Tom was sentenced to life at Alcatraz. One day when the guards were busy searching for another inmate, Tom scaled down the rocks and climbed aboard a small boat. The authorities believed his girlfriend may have aided his escape by having the boat waiting. Neither Tom nor his girlfriend were located.

Months later, Harry Ford and Henry Betty, two military prisoners, escaped while working at Fort Baker. They knocked out a guard and took off running. They were captured hours later after a hail of gunshots rang out by the guards. The guards were on orders to shoot to kill after two other military prisoners had successfully escaped weeks before.

In 1903, four military prisoners were sent to Alcatraz. While working at Fort Mason, the prisoners overpowered a guard and took off running. One of the prisoners was quickly captured, but the other three were never located.

Later that year, three prisoners used the print shop to create their own release documents. Their plan was successful to the point they were officially released and placed on a boat to San Francisco. It was only after they landed that the prison officials realized the documents had been forged. They located one of the prisoners and he was returned to Alcatraz. The other two prisoners were never found.

In 1908, the oil barge *Santiago* picked up a military prisoner who was clinging to a plank of wood. He admitted he had escaped from Alcatraz. The oil barge took him to Monterey Bay. Upon seeing soldiers waiting for him, the prisoner tossed a rope over the side of the barge and slid down the rope to his freedom. The soldiers were not able to locate him.

In 1909, the government put the prisoners to work building a new cellhouse that could house 600 inmates. They also built a hospital, a mess hall, and many outbuildings. By the time the construction was completed three years later, it was thought to be inescapable. No sooner had the authorities boasted that no inmate could possibly escape the fortress than the escapes began.

Thomas Franey and Michael Mullin sawed their way out of their cell and escaped on a raft. They made it to a cave where they hid under driftwood for four days. Michael ducked out of the cave during the fourth night to get water for Thomas, who was close to death. Thomas was spotted and both men were returned to Alcatraz.

Charles Roberts, age twenty-six, John Howington, age nineteen, and Robert Hanna, age thirty-two, used a fine-tooth steel saw on the bars to their cells and made their escape under the cover of darkness. Boats patrolled the water surrounding Alcatraz all night before the trio was spotted on a makeshift log raft at 5 a.m. Robert Hanna was serving a ten-year sentence, but the other two were due to be released in a matter of weeks.

Inmate Virgil Tolliver was serving a twenty-year sentence at the military prison for desertion. In 1920, he stole a woman's dress that belonged to an officer's wife who lived on the island. He managed to walk past the guards and get on an Alcatraz boat. Once the boat arrived in Fort Mason, he walked past another set of guards and remained free for three months before being located in Oregon and returned to Alcatraz.

In 1926, escapee George Berryman, age twenty-two, plunged into the frigid waters and attempted to swim to the mainland. He was never found, and the authorities believed he drowned in the strong tide.

In 1929, Frank LaBarron managed to jump into the water but was picked up almost immediately by an army tugboat. Frank was returned to the barracks and placed in solitary confinement.

The following year, Jack Allen plunged into the frigid waters and was never found. Colonel M. G. Cralie commented: "If he swan for it, he most certainly drowned. He was only an ordinary swimmer."

Later that year, William Smith, Howard Munson, and Donald Rinard managed to make it to the water, but they soon began calling out for help. They were quickly rescued and returned to the barracks.

Over the years, there were other escape attempts. Some of the escapees were rescued; others were never located.

In 1933, the U.S. Army turned Alcatraz over to the U.S. Department of Justice to be used as a maximum-security prison. James A. Johnston was hired as the prison warden at a salary of $6,600 per year. His job was to guard what the government referred to as "the incorrigibles." Warden Johnston had previously been a warden at both San Quentin and Folsom prisons. He told the media:

> The maximum of security of its inmates is the main objective of this prison. The worst of the worst prisoners will be kept here. And they will be kept here, as the government has spent several hundred thousand dollars to make this prison "escape proof." Trained guards from Atlanta, Leavenworth, McNeil's and other government prisons have been transferred here to assure a crack crop of custodians.[1]

In 1934, the first prisoners arrived at Alcatraz, or as it was commonly known "America's Devils Island." The press continually referred to the prison as "escape proof." Before the prison opened, the government installed an "electrical field" that would sound an alarm if an inmate ventured too close to the edge of the island. The government installed "ray machines" that could detect if a prisoner was carrying any metal. They also brought in dogs that were trained to detect and attack any prisoner who tried to escape. The electric gates were controlled from the prison towers. Signs were posted around the island warning boats to stay 300 feet away. Communication from the prison to the Coast Guard was conducted by two-way radios. Searchlights spanned the island. Tear gas and machine guns were staged throughout the prison. Prison guards walked along outside catwalks carrying machine guns.

The prison was complete with a surgery center and hospital, an assembly hall with a stage, a library, a large laundry, a shoe shop, a clothing factory, mess hall, kitchen, garden, and a baseball field. Although the prison could house 600 inmates, the government only transferred 200 inmates, due to the severity of the inmates chosen to be imprisoned at Alcatraz.

Some of the more well-known inmates who were the first to arrive included Al Capone, Albert Bates, and George "Machine Gun" Kelly. All 200 of the new arrivals were transferred from other federal prisons under great secrecy. They were transported in a special armored train. Once the train reached San

Francisco, the train car was placed on a barge and transported to Alcatraz. A Coast Guard cutter with personnel armed with guns sailed alongside the barge.

The guards lived in housing on the island. Many of them had wives and children who lived with them. All of the guards were expected to be adept at wrestling, boxing, and jiu-jitsu. They were also expected to be educated in criminology and psychology.

The inmates were not allowed to read newspapers or magazines, and visitors were not allowed at the prison. Those who did not follow the rules found themselves in the "dungeons." The dungeons were located under the buildings where there was no daylight.

Soon after Alcatraz opened, inmate John Stadig managed to escape as he was being transported from a court appearance in Portland, Oregon, back to Alcatraz. John overpowered the U.S. Marshals on the train and dove out a window while the train was moving. John had escaped four times from other federal prisons while serving time for counterfeiting. While serving a sentence at McNeil Federal Prison in Washington state, John stole a work truck and drove through a barbed-wire fence. Once he realized he could not get off the island, he hid at a farmhouse on the island until he was discovered. John was sent to Alcatraz after being classified as one of the "ten toughest prisoners."

The authorities located John in Concord six days after his escape from the moving train. The police fired one shot and he surrendered. John told reporters that life at Alcatraz was "hell on earth." He cited the discipline and horrible food at the prison. He blamed Warden Johnston and the guards for giving Al Capone preferential treatment. Warden Johnston denied the accusation emphasizing, "Every cell is identical and every prisoner is given identical treatment, with no exceptions for Capone or anyone else."

Joseph "Joe" Bowers, age forty, was facing twenty-one years at Alcatraz for mail robbery when he made the decision to escape in 1936. Prison guards spotted Joe as he scaled a barbed-wire fence by the prison's incinerator where he was working. The guards opened fire and Joe fell to his death.

One of the first prisoners to be released from Alcatraz was Verrill Rapp. He told the media that Al Capone had been placed in solitary confinement after a fight broke out with another inmate while they were working in the prison laundry. Verrill described solitary confinement as being shackled twenty-four hours a day with the prisoner's hands chained to the ceiling during the day. He described brutal beatings by the guards.

Verrill went on to say: "We were allowed to talk five minutes in the mornings, five minutes in the afternoon, and to smoke five minutes in the afternoon. The rest is silence-no talk in cells or lines." He added: "Sixty per cent of the convicts work, and forty per cent are idle, with a rotating system used." Verrill said they were allowed to play softball for two hours each Saturday and Sunday.

A prison riot took place at Alcatraz in 1936. An estimated 100 inmates staged a strike claiming inhuman rules at the prison. The prison guards rounded up the ringleaders and placed them in the dungeon, and the other men returned to work.

Newspapers across the country continued to run articles claiming that Alcatraz was "escape proof." Three years after Alcatraz opened, Theodore "Ted" Cole, age twenty-five, and Ralph Roe, age twenty-nine, decided to put that theory to the test. On December 16, 1937, during one of the foggiest nights in years, the two prisoners managed to climb through a window that was 9 inches high and 18 inches long. The window had bars that crisscrossed the expanse of the window.

Warden Johnston explained to the media that the men must have been sawing the bars over a long period of time. He did not know how the duo obtained a sharp instrument or went undetected. He went on to explain that once Ted and Ralph got out the window, they stole a wrench from the machine shop and used it to pry open a gate which led to a 20-foot cliff. Warden Johnston initially believed the prisoners were hiding somewhere on the island and had not plunged into the water. However, after personally searching the island for hours, Warden Johnston said he believed the men either drowned or had outside help and had been picked up in a boat. However, he added: "Serving terms tantamount to life imprisonment, it is my belief they decided to take a desperate chance and that they had no outside aid."

Federal, state, and local police boats joined the Coast Guard in searching for the two escapees. Every inch of the 12-acre island was searched without any answers. The fog was so dense that the guards were not able to see the Coast Guard boats approaching the island.

FBI Special Agent N. L. Pieper assured reporters that they would continue to search for the escapees, "until the men are found, dead or alive." He emphasized: "Those who harbor the convicts will be prosecuted just as hard as the convicts themselves."

As news spread of the escape, tips flooded in claiming the men were in various locations, but none of the tips ever panned out. There were reports that a cabin cruiser vessel and a rowboat had been sighted near Alcatraz the night of the escape. After investigating the tip, the FBI concluded the boats were not involved in the escape.

Ted and Ralph were from Oklahoma and had served time together at the Oklahoma State Penitentiary in McAlester, Oklahoma. They were transported together to Alcatraz. Warden Jess Dunn of the Oklahoma State Penitentiary recalled that shortly before Ted was to be transferred, he said: "I don't think I'll like the island and doubt if I'll stay there long enough to be bored."

When Ted was seventeen years old, he was sent to the Oklahoma State Penitentiary after stints in a reformatory. While in prison, he attempted to scale a fence and was shot in the leg. The following year, he admitted he murdered his cellmate, William Pritchett, by stabbing him twenty-seven times. While awaiting his murder trial, Ted concealed himself in a bag of laundry and escaped when the laundry truck left the prison grounds. Once on the outside, Ted kidnapped J. A. Rutherford, a merchant in Cushing, Oklahoma, and forced him to drive to Springfield, Illinois. Once in Springfield, Ted disappeared and was not seen again until he was arrested in Dallas, Texas. Ted was returned to Oklahoma. While incarcerated in a county jail awaiting his murder trial and his new charges, Ted tied a bed sheet around the "saw-proof" bars and pulled hard enough to loosen the bars. He attempted to escape by concealing himself in a trash can that was carried out of the jail before the guards found him hidden among the garbage. One of the jail staff commented: "Cole would work the jail locks better than the people who built the place."

After the escape, the media questioned Oklahoma City Sheriff Stanley Rogers about his memories of Ted. He stated: "Cole is like a greased pig and I wouldn't be surprised at anything he could do."

Ted was sent to Alcatraz for fifty years for the kidnapping. Ralph was serving a ninety-nine-year sentence for robbing a bank in Muskogee, Oklahoma.

The dawn of the new year and every year since then did not bring any answers as to the fate of Ralph and Ted. As to whether Ralph and Ted survived, or died trying, remains a mystery to this day.

Buoyed by the possibility that Ralph and Ted successfully escaped, three inmates made their own bid for freedom five months later.

Rufus Franklin, who was convicted of murder in Alabama, James Lucas, who was convicted of bank robbery, and Thomas Limerick, who was also convicted of bank robbery, were working in the wood shop when they grabbed a hammer and bludgeoned prison guard Royal C. Cline, age thirty-six. Prison guard Harold Stites came to the rescue of Royal and the inmates fled.

The inmates ran to a window and managed to get up to the top of the factory building before a guard saw them and opened fire. Rufus was captured after being shot in the shoulder. Thomas was shot in the head and died at the scene. James hid from the gunfire but surrendered within minutes.

Prison guard Cline was rushed to the Marine Hospital but never regained consciousness and succumbed to his injuries. His wife lived with him on the island. Prison guards who worked inside the prison were not armed, in an effort to prevent an inmate from grabbing their weapon. The guards who worked in the towers and patrolled the catwalks and grounds retrieved their firearms from an armory that was not assessable from the inside of the prison.

Rufus and James were convicted of first-degree murder for the murder of Cline after a federal trial was held in San Francisco. They were placed in isolation at Alcatraz.

The following year saw a brazen attempt by five inmates to escape. Rufus McCain, age thirty-six, Henri Young, age twenty-eight, William Martin, age twenty-five, Dale Stamphill, age twenty-seven, and Arthur "Doc" Barker, age forty, attempted to escape from Alcatraz.

The five used a file to saw through the bars on their cells, forced open a door, slithered through a window, dropped 10 feet to the ground, and made their way to the water's edge. At 4 a.m., a guard saw the empty cells and sounded the alarm. Every searchlight was turned on, but the fog was so thick that the guards could barely see in front of them. The San Francisco Police Department was notified, and they immediately began guarding the shore. U.S. Army and Coast Guard boats patrolled the choppy waters of the San Francisco Bay while other soldiers stationed themselves along the shore.

As guards got closer to the water's edge, they spotted Doc and Dale preparing to drop to the water. Warnings were given and shots rang out. Doc was fatally wounded, and Dale was shot in both legs. Rufus and Henri surrendered when the guards shouted at them to stop. William was located near the rocks by the water's edge. He was bleeding from sliding down the rocks.

There was a time that the FBI named Doc as Public Enemy Number 1 for his far-reaching crimes. Doc's mother, "Ma" Barker, and Doc's brothers all had a long criminal history. Doc was serving a life sentence at Alcatraz after committing a series of crimes stretching over two decades.

The residents of San Francisco and the surrounding areas were becoming increasingly concerned about the escapes from the "escape proof" federal prison where the nation's most dangerous criminals were housed. Equally concerned was U.S. Prison Director James Bennett, who made a personal visit to the island after the five made their getaway. Director Bennett said experiments were being done on a new type of steel that might be beneficial for Alcatraz. He also recommended adding sodium vapor lights to assist the guards during times of heavy fog after Warden Johnston described the fog as being "like a mass of wool" the night the five attempted to escape.

The entire prison was searched for the saws that the five inmates used to saw through their cell bars, but they were never located. When reporters questioned the warden about how five inmates obtained saws, he replied:

> It is possible that the saws may have been brought into the prison kitchen welded to cans containing food. These cans do not pass through the electric metal detectors.
>
> One must not lose sight of the fact that these prisoners always are thinking of methods of escape. One of those who participated in the recent getaway attempt is an expert safecracker. He told me that there isn't very much a man can do that another man can't undo. We're going to try to disprove this statement.[2]

Two years later, four inmates made their bid for freedom. Lloyd Bardoll, Joseph Cretzer, Arnold Thomas Kyle, and Sam Schokleu were spotted by a guard as they attempted to cut through the steel bars in the mat shop. They overpowered the first three guards who tried to stop them, but they were stopped when additional guards arrived to assist.

Lloyd was serving time for bank robbery. Joseph had previously escaped from McNeil Federal Prison and killed a U.S. Marshal while on the run. Arnold was Joseph's brother-in-law and was serving time for assisting Joseph escape from McNeil Federal Prison. Sam was sent to Alcatraz for kidnapping and robbing a bank.

Kay Wallace, who was Joseph's wife and Arnold's sister, was located in Oakland and taken in for questioning to determine if she was involved in the escape attempt. She was released after it was determined she had not aided their escape attempt.

Months later, inmate John Bayless was working on a garbage detail when the guards saw him running for the water's edge. The guards sounded the alarm and shouted for John to stop. John gave up and surrendered. Warden Johnston told reporters: "Bayless didn't get a chance to swim. He came back quietly when he heard the officer yell."

John was not content to give up on his dream of escaping. While in court the following year, while arguing for a writ of *habeas corpus*, John made a run for the courthouse door. A U.S. Marshal quickly put an end to his bid for freedom and John was returned to Alcatraz.

Undeterred by the lack of successful escape attempts, James Boardman, age twenty-four, Harold Martin Brest, age thirty-one, Fred Hunter, age forty-three, and Floyd Hamilton, age thirty-six, overpowered two guards in 1943. They bound and gagged the guards before leaping out a window and running to the edge of the island. One of the prison guards, Henry Weinhold, managed to get loose and sound the alarm. The four men were spotted by guards in towers who opened fire. James was shot as he reached the water.

A patrol boat spotted James and Harold in the water. As the boat approached the two men, Harold let go of James, who by that time was dead, and his body was carried off by the current.

Fred was located hiding in a cave on the island. Three days later, Floyd was located in the industrial shop on the island. He admitted he spent the first two days holed up in a cave before climbing up the rocks and entering the industrial shop through a window.

Harold had been released from Alcatraz two years before under a writ of *habeas corpus*. His freedom was short lived, and he was returned to Alcatraz for life imprisonment plus fifty-five years for kidnapping and bank robbery.

Four months later, Ted Huron Walters, age thirty, made an attempt at freedom. Ted snuck out of the prison laundry, scaled a barbed-wire fence, and was almost to the water when he was grabbed by a guard. Ted was serving a thirty-year sentence for bank robbery.

In 1945, John Giles, age fifty, stole an army uniform from the prison laundry and made his way to the water where he boarded an army vessel. When the guards discovered he was missing at a head count, the alarm was sounded. As the army boat docked at Angel Island, army officials were waiting for him, and he was returned to Alcatraz to finish his twenty-year sentence for robbing a post office in Salt Lake City.

One of the most dramatic escape attempts became known as the "Battle of Alcatraz." On May 2, 1946 at 2:30 p.m., orderly inmate Bernard Paul Coy was cleaning the floor in cell block C. Directly above cell block C was a gun gallery. The gun galleries did not open to the inside of the prison. The guards could only access the gun galleries through two armored doors from outside of the prison.

Bernard climbed up on a radiator and jumped from the radiator and grabbed the bottom rung of a ladder and began climbing. He reached the top where the bars curved to the wall. He inserted a metal spreader he had made. The spreader consisted of about a dozen pieces of connections from prison toilets that had been screwed together. Bernard used the spreader and a pair of pliers he had stolen to create a gap in the metal bars that measured 7 inches by 18 inches.

Bernard managed to squirm through the opening and contacted prison guard Bert Burch who was working in the gun gallery. Bernard knocked Bert out and stole his weapons, coat, and keys. Bernard returned to cell block C through the opening that he made.

Bernard immediately freed Joseph Paul Cretzer, Miran Thompson, Louis Flelsher, Sam Shockley, Myron Edgar Franklin, Clarence Carnes, and Marvin Franklin Hubbard.

Bernard threw a switch that opened all of the cell blocks. Most of the inmates remained in their cells, but those who ran for freedom met up with Bernard. The inmates grabbed ammunition and firearms and made their way through the prison, firing at every guard they saw.

Within minutes, two prison guards were killed and fourteen were wounded. The guards who were not held captive sounded the alarm and patrolled the hallways, roof, and all exit points. Warden Johnston sent teletypes to all nearby law enforcement and military requesting their assistance.

All buildings went into lockdown when the alarm sounded. That included the prison hospital where a dentist and a medical doctor were working before the attack. They were not able to get out of the building to assist the wounded guards. Warden Johnston requested nurses and doctors from nearby hospitals respond to the island.

The local U.S. Marine Corps left immediately from Treasure Island and landed on Alcatraz. They rescued the injured prison guards and guarded the prisoners who were not involved in the uprising. The wounded guards were rushed to two hospitals in San Francisco.

The Coast Guard sent five boats to patrol the waters surrounding the island. The U.S. Navy provided two boats, a contingent of sailors, and an airplane to assist. All local law enforcement provided officers. The U.S. Air Corps and the U.S. Army immediately sent personnel to help on the island. The San Francisco Police Department sent their best marksmen along with Tommy guns, tear gas guns, automatic shotguns, and a large assortment of rifles and pistols.

Federal prison guards travelled from McNeil Federal Prison in Washington state, Leavenworth Federal Prison in Kansas, and Englewood Federal Prison in Colorado to assist at Alcatraz. San Quentin Prison sent guards to Alcatraz to assist.

For hours, gunfire blasted through the complex. As the hours dragged on, it appeared the battle was confined to the west wing of the main cell block. The guards walking the catwalks fired their weapons at windows above their heads. When they ran out of ammunition, they ran to reload, trying to stay out of view of the prisoners.

Minutes before taking his final breath, prison guard William Miller identified Joseph as the inmate who shot him.

One of the guards who died instantly from being shot with a machine gun was Harold Stites. Eight years before, Harold tried to save prison guard Royal Cline when he was shot during an escape attempt.

It became apparent that, in addition to Bernard, the other ringleaders for the takeover were Joseph Paul Cretzer, age thirty-five, Miran Thompson, age twenty-nine, Louis Flelsher, Sam Shockley, age thirty-six, Myron Edgar Franklin, age twenty-nine, Clarence Carnes, age nineteen, and Marvin Franklin Hubbard, age thirty-four.

Joseph had attempted to escape from Alcatraz in 1941. He was serving time at Alcatraz for robbing a bank and killing a U.S. Marshal. The FBI once named Joseph "Public Enemy No. 5." They also named Joseph and his brother-in-law, Arnold Kyle, "The Nation's No. 1 bank robbing team."

Bernard was serving a twenty-five sentence for committing a robbery in Kentucky. Miran was serving ninety-nine years on a kidnapping charge and life imprisonment for murdering a police officer in Amarillo, Texas. Sam was serving life imprisonment for kidnapping and robbing a bank in Muskogee, Oklahoma. Marvin was sent to Alcatraz after being sentenced to thirty years for a kidnapping that took place in Chattanooga, Tennessee. Clarence was sentenced to ninety-nine years for a kidnapping and murder he committed in Oklahoma. Louis had a long history of crimes as a gang member in Detroit, Michigan. He was serving thirty years at Alcatraz for possession of unregistered machine guns.

Early on the inmates seized a kitchen and took food supplies. The guards were able to take the kitchen back when more guards arrived on the island.

Warden Johnston sent a telegram to local newspapers stating:

> Serious trouble. Convict has machine gun in cell house. Have issued riot call.
> Placed armed guards at strategic locations.
> Most of our officers are imprisoned in cell house.

Cannot tell extent of injuries suffered by our officers or amount of damage done.

Will give you more information later in the day when we get control.

When the news of the trouble at Alcatraz hit the newspapers and radios, thousands of onlookers lined the shores of the San Francisco Bay trying to catch a glimpse of what was happening on the island. Those living in the hills waited and watched from their perch. Thousands of people lined the Golden Gate Bridge trying to see what was happening on "The Rock." The police were strained trying to deal with traffic jams as people tried to get to a spot where they could catch a view of Alcatraz. Some of the onlookers who owned a pair of binoculars became entrepreneurs and charged onlookers "10 cents a look."

When Alcatraz went into lockdown, all boat transportation was suspended to Alcatraz. The children of the guards who attended school in San Francisco were left stranded, as were many of the guards' wives who were in San Francisco when Alcatraz went into lockdown. They had to scramble to find their children and locate accommodations.

The military drilled holes in the roof where the inmates were holed up. They dropped 150 grenades through the holes.

The military sent additional personnel to the island. They also replenished the stock of weapons and ammunition. On the second day of the siege, Warden Johnson requested 100 bazookas, 720 carbine cartridges, 288 grenade adapters for rifles, 1,000 fragmentation grenades, 300 smoke grenades, and 15-pound shaped charges.

After forty hours of the siege, there were nine inmates holding out. Warden Johnston reached the holdouts over the prison telephone and asked if they were ready to surrender. They quickly replied, "Hell no—if we surrender, you'll hang us."

One prison authority told a reporter, "We're just waiting. It's their move next." He assured the reporter, "We have completely prevented the mass escape plot. Now we must secure the firearms and the men who have them."

Later that day, an inmate phoned Warden J. A. Johnston and stated: "We want to make a deal." Warden Johnston informed the inmate: "We'll make a deal when you throw your weapons and ammunition out." The inmate ended the telephone call and there was no further communication.

Soon after, sharpshooters from Leavenworth prison stormed cell block C and discovered three of the ringleaders, Joseph, Bernard, and Marvin, deceased. They rounded up the other escapees who were holed up with the deceased inmates and placed them in solitary confinement. The prison authorities believed the ringleaders died from the grenades the military dropped through the hole they cut in the roof and/or from machine-gun fire done by the U.S. Marines.

Warden Johnston assured the press, "it seems quite certain that no prisoner escaped." There were no other casualties among the inmates.

Prison guard Robert Baker, who was shot three times in the leg and foot, told reporters about the first few minutes: "That Coy was the leader. But Cretzer seemed to get the most pleasure out of shooting people down. He stuck his gun in the door and laughed. He always hated [prison guard] Simpson."

Prison guard Harry Cochran was at home in San Rafael enjoying a day off when he heard about the riot over the radio. He took the first boat he could and landed on the island. Harry later told reporters: "I rushed toward 'D' block with a .45. Stites was covering me as I ducked and ran toward the penned up cons. Then I got shot. Stites went on after them." Minutes later, Stites was shot and killed.

Prison guard Robert Baker later told reporters about the first moments of the uprising. He said he was in the front office of the prison when he heard that a riot was breaking out:

> We ran toward the cell block, and that was where ten or twelve of 'em jumped us. We were caught off guard.
>
> I saw "Crazy" Thompson—he's crazy all right, like a fox—run to the gun gallery and take an automatic rifle. He threatened us, but I didn't ever see him shoot.
>
> I was shot down in cold blood by Cretzer, a lifer, along with two other guards.

Robert spoke of feigning death for ten hours crammed into a jail cell. He explained that Joseph just laughed when "someone suggested they hold us as hostages." Joseph's response, according to Robert, was, "We don't need hostages. We're not going to make agreements. We want the keys."

Robert went on to say:

> Someone said Miller [prison guard William A. Miller] had the keys. They threw Miller on a bench, punching and kicking him and demanding he gave them up. Miller took it as long as he could and finally surrendered some keys, but he held out the most important—the key to the back gate.
>
> He wouldn't tell where it was and finally he passed out from the torture. The shooting had started by then and Coy made a break for the back gate. He didn't get out.
>
> The others seemed to go crazy. Thompson brandished a rifle. The whole mass of them rushed us. They jammed us into two cells. I was in the one with Lt. J.H. Simpson and Carl Sundstrom. In the other cell were Capt. H.W. Weinhold, Ernest Logerson, Miller and Cecil Corwin.
>
> I don't know who fired into the other cell, but Cretzer stood at the door to the cell I was in and went wild. He emptied a .45 automatic into us.
>
> It happened in a second—there wasn't time to think of falling to the floor. The air seemed full of bullets. Simpson stood on the bed. Two bullets hit him in the chest and he fell flat on the cot.

Before I could wiggle under the bed, a bullet got me and dropped me. Sundstrom fell to the floor behind me as bullets poured in, but he was unhurt. I thought Cretzer would come in and finish us off. But he left.

I lay there for 10 hours with blood splashing from my wound. The floor was cold and I didn't pass out. Sundstrom hugged the floor without a sound. I could hear Simpson moaning. We didn't dare help him. The convicts kept coming back and looking in.

When Cretzer said he didn't want hostages, a con said, "Let's kill these witnesses. We don't want witnesses."

Coy was one convict who did plenty of damage during it all. I saw him pick off three guards with as many shots during the start of the fight in the cell tiers.[3]

Robert was asked by a reporter if there had been any indications that a riot was about to take place. He replied: "They're always threatening to do something, but we don't pay any attention to that. They get maddest about having their mail censored."

Prison guard Fred Richberger told reporters: "I was hit in both legs, but it all happened so quickly I didn't even know where the shots came from."

Prison guard Harold Stites' wife, Bessie, and their three children joined an overflowing crowd at a service for Harold at a chapel in San Francisco. Harold was buried in the Golden Gate Cemetery with full military honors for his service in World War I.

Prison guard William Miller's body was transported to Philadelphia for burial. William had transferred from a federal prison in Pennsylvania one year before he was killed at Alcatraz. When the public learned there were no government funds to pay for William's transportation to Philadelphia, or for his funeral, they immediately sent in contributions. Warden Johnston announced within hours almost $1,000 had been raised. The warden told reporters: "I never saw anything like it. Why, some of the men pitched in their pay checks intact, they were so distressed over the fact that the Government isn't going to pay the bills for these guards." The contributions totaled $7,500, and was split between the families.

Later the National Council of Prison Employees was instrumental in enacting laws to provide compensation for the families of prison employees killed in the line of duty.

A federal grand jury found inmates Miran and Sam guilty of first-degree murder for the death of prison guards William Miller and Harold Stites. They were sentenced to die at San Quentin Prison. Clarence received a life imprisonment sentence instead of the death penalty because of his age. Although the three men never fired a weapon, they were tried for being co-conspirators in the escape plan.

When Miran and Sam were led inside San Quentin Prison, they were shackled and handcuffed, but they had their fingers crossed. They explained to the waiting reporters that they were hoping they would receive clemency. All of their appeals were denied, and an execution date was set.

The day before they were to be executed, Miran and Sam appeared before a group of reporters at San Quentin. Sam was not interested in the proceedings and asked to be taken back to his cell. Miran took the opportunity to show the reporters his eighteen-page appeal:

> You see this. A copy of the plea I sent right to the top: to President Truman. I asked for clemency, see; told him the whole story.
>
> The warden here says it was turned down yesterday by some big guy in Washington. I don't believe it. They haven't sent me the official word.
>
> Not bad for a guy who just got through the third grade. It's the story. I've done a lot of things in my day; been in a lot of pens. Alcatraz was the only one that'd hold me.
>
> But never murder. And in the testimony they said I swore while the break was going on. Not me. Look, I've got a wife and kids; I'm a God-fearing man. No swearing; no murder.
>
> You want to know who killed Miller? Cretzer did it. That guy was crazy.
>
> The whole time the fight was going on he had the key that would have let us out of the cell block. But he was nuts. He forced me out of my cell.
>
> And when they found him dead afterwards you could tell he was the guy that did the killing. He was down like this (Thompson crouched dramatically in a corner of the cell) with the gun still frozen in his hands.
>
> Tell you what I told the President. If he'll let me take truth serum and force Warden Johnston and some of those guards to take it too-then we'll see who's telling the truth. That's all.[4]

At 10:00 a.m. on December 2, 1948, Miran and Sam were executed at San Quentin Prison.

Over the years, there were more escapes until the government shut down the prison in 1963 citing the high cost of maintaining the aged buildings and transporting supplies to the island. The previous year, Frank Morris and brothers John and Clarence Anglin escaped from Alcatraz and were never seen or heard from again.

16
Albert LeRoy Jones

Mrytle Mae Nielson, age forty-six, was at her house on W. 12th Avenue in Chico with her nineteen-year-old daughter, Betty, and a friend of the family, Barbara Searle, age five, on July 16, 1946. In the early afternoon, Albert LeRoy Jones, age fourteen, knocked on their door and asked to come in.

Albert attended Central Grammar School where Betty worked as a secretary. Betty let Albert into the house where Mrytle was canning apricots and Barbara was playing with watercolors.

Albert was carrying a German Luger firearm and said he was going to do some work on the weapon. He went into the living room and turned on the radio. Albert then walked back into the kitchen and leaned against the doorway. Myrtle asked him if he wanted some water and a cookie. Albert nodded in agreement, and as Myrtle turned her back to retrieve the cookie and water, Albert brought the gun up and shot Myrtle in the back. She fell to the floor, but even as she lay bleeding, she said: "Albert you did not hurt me. Run away now and I'll say it was an accident." To which Albert replied: "That's a lie! You are too hurt." Albert grabbed some apricots and stuffed them in Myrtle's mouth and gagged her with a towel. He bound Betty and Barbara before ransacking the house.

Betty continually begged Albert to let her call for medical assistance for her mother, but Albert refused. He picked up some knives and told Betty: "I could kill you with these and not make any noise but I'm better at strangling." He then informed them that he had murdered a classmate, Patricia Crandall, four weeks ago.

Finally, after two hours of begging, Albert agreed to allow Betty to phone her father, Harold Nielson, at his workplace. Betty frantically told her father to come home right away.

Harold rushed home, and as he entered the house, Albert fired his weapon directly at Harold. The bullet grazed Harold's body and he began physically fighting with Albert. A neighbor of the Nielsons', Latricia Overton, age seventeen, heard the gunshot and rushed over to the Nielsons' house. She managed to untie Betty and Barbara before calling the police and then calling for an ambulance.

Mrytle underwent a three-hour-long surgery at Enloe Hospital. She remained in critical condition and died less than twenty-four hours after being shot. The doctors believed if she had received medical care earlier, she would have lived. Mrytle lost a great deal of blood during the two hours she was forced to remain on the kitchen floor.

For nine years Mrytle operated a home-away-from-home for male students at Chico State College (University). When word spread through the town of Chico that Mrytle was critically injured, the men she had taken care of for years rushed to the hospital and donated blood. Every officer with the Chico Police Department offered to donate blood.

Myrtle and Harold had two daughters, Betty and Ona. The family had lived in Chico for ten years. Harold had worked for Lapham Motors since arriving in Chico.

Constable Roy Knapp with the Chico Police Department arrested Albert and took him to the city jail located within the police station on Main Street. It was there that Albert confessed to the events at the Nielsons' house, and also confessed to murdering sixteen-year-old Patricia Crandall a month before.

Albert explained Patricia was a friend of his sister, Emma, and he also knew Patricia from school. Patricia lived at 15th and Chestnut Streets with her parents. He said on the day he killed Patricia, they argued about his mistreatment of her cat. She was angry at him and wanted him to leave her house, and that is when he strangled her.

In a quiet voice, Albert admitted to strangling Patricia: "I twisted her arm and forced her to go into the bedroom, where I choked her with a cloth. I didn't feel sorry for her then. I do now."

Albert said Patricia tried to cry out for help while he was choking her. He admitted that after she stopped moving, he placed newspapers and magazines around her body. He located a bottle of lighter fluid and poured it on the newspapers and ignited the fire. Albert added: "Her hair was afire when I looked last." He admitted he ransacked the house and stole a pen and pencil set Patricia had given to her father for Father's Day.

The police said Albert had been questioned at length about the fire because he was seen in the neighborhood the afternoon of the fire. They explained no one had ever been charged with the arson due to the fire destroying the evidence. The autopsy showed Patricia died from the burns that consumed her body.

Deputy Sheriff Clarence Hayes transported Albert to the Butte County jail in Oroville. Once in a jail cell, he requested something to read. The staff brought him newspapers and magazines. Deputy District Attorney Raymond Leonard interviewed Albert at the jail.

Albert explained to Deputy District Attorney Leonard that he stole the firearm from his uncle, William Atteberry. He said he had never fired the weapon before. When asked if he planned to kill anyone else, Albert readily admitted he planned to murder a classmate, Harlan Hume, age fourteen. He expanded by saying

Harlan was the only boy that ever befriended him and invited him over for dinner. When asked if he liked Harlan, Albert matter-of-factly said: "Yes, I liked him, but I wanted to kill him." Albert referred to Harlan as his "best friend." He went on to say: "I wasn't mad at him. I just thought about killing him. I was going to push him into the creek and drown him."

The District Attorney's Office charged Albert with two counts of first-degree murder, one count of attempted murder, and two counts of assault with a deadly weapon with the intent to commit murder. Albert signed a complete confession regarding the murder of Patricia and the shooting at the Nielsons' home.

In Albert's confession, he admitted to stealing jewelry and an Eversharp pencil and pen set from the Crandalls' house and stashing it along Lindo Channel. The following day, Deputy District Attorney Leonard and Deputy Sheriff Ray Head took Albert to the area where he said he stashed the stolen goods. They were able to recover a wristwatch, the Eversharp pencil, and some loose pearls.

From his jail cell, Albert spoke to Chico Enterprise Record reporter Paul Thompson. During the interview, Albert said he did not feel any remorse when he saw Patricia dying in front of him. When asked about the events that took place at the Nielsons' house, Albert replied: "I wanted to rob them and take Mr. Nielson's car. I wanted to leave Chico and get out of town, up north, maybe. I was going to shoot whoever I had to. I was waiting for Nielson to come home and I planned to shoot him and take the car."[1]

When asked about his background, Albert replied:

> I couldn't get along with any of my brothers or sisters. I couldn't get along with my mother. None of the kids at school seemed to like me. I don't know why, I guess I didn't have any friends.
>
> Maybe I was pretty good before this year, but I sorta fell down. I did manage to get into high school, and I wanted to go to high school.[2]

Albert's mother, Ada Jones, age thirty-one, assured reporters: "Albert couldn't have done this and part of the time he didn't know what he was doing—he was sick." Albert's younger brother, Tommie, age ten, said: "I just don't know what to believe … I just don't know what to believe." Albert's sister, Emma, age sixteen, sobbed when she heard the news that her brother was responsible for murdering her friend, Patricia. Albert's other sister, Delia, age twelve, told reporters: "They've questioned him so darn much he doesn't know what he's talking about." Albert's father died when he was young. His mother remarried, but that relationship ended when Albert was eleven years old.

The would-be victim, Harlan Hume, told reporters:

> I used to go play with Albert at his house some time ago. I played with him because it seemed no one else would, and he didn't have any friends. I didn't

like the idea of the rest of the boys acting the way they did just because Albert seemed different. That's the reason I was nice to him. I felt sorry for him. I haven't played with him or talked to him for sometime now. But one time I went to a movie with him and one time I invited him to dinner. I'm not quite sure whether he came or not.[3]

Albert was arraigned before Justice of the Peace S. P. Robbins. During the arraignment, arrangements were made to have Albert examined by a psychiatrist. Albert's mother informed the court she had accepted an offer from the Carr and Donelson law firm in Sacramento to represent Albert free of charge. The California Bar Association agreed to the offer. Ada told the court a local attorney wanted a $2,500 retainer and expected the case would cost between $5,000 and 10,000. Ada explained she worked at the Chico Laundry and did not have the funds to provide her son with legal counsel.

After the arraignment, the police were leading Albert out of the courtroom, when Patricia's mother blocked their path and demanded, "Why did you kill Pat?" A moment later, another woman in the courtroom shouted: "Don't ask him that! He's a murderer and a liar!"

Suddenly, Albert's mother rushed the woman screaming, "You lie!" Before deputies with the Butte County Sheriff's Office could separate the women, Ada got away and ran after her son before collapsing in hysterics outside the courtroom.

Two months later, Superior Court Judge Harry Delrup ordered that Albert be sent to the Mendocino State Hospital for a period of ninety days so that an assessment could be completed.

Dr. Walter Rappaport of the Mendocino State Hospital reported to Judge Delrup that Albert was "sane and competent, but a psychopathic delinquent." He explained: "Treatment under present conditions will result in no benefit, but we believe there might be some chance for improvement after the murder charge has been disposed of."

The following year, Judge Delrup denied a change of venue request by the defense team, and the trial got underway with more than 100 spectators. Butte County District Attorney Jack McPherson represented the state of California.

The Crandalls' landlord, Mrs. Banta, informed the jury that she saw Albert at the Crandalls' house the day of the fire and for two days leading up to the fire. She recalled seeing Patricia shaking her head "no" for several minutes before she witnessed Albert leave on his bicycle the day of the fire. She said a short time later, she and her husband saw flames coming from the Crandalls' house. She described how her husband tried to put the fire out using a garden hose.

Patricia's father took the stand and identified the items stolen from his house that had been recovered along Lindo Channel. He told the jury the only time he ever saw Albert was two days before Patricia was murdered when Albert was at their house.

Harold took the stand and told the panel of jurists that when he arrived home after Betty called him at work, Betty shouted: "He shot mom!" He said Myrtle was conscious and warned him: "He's in the bedroom and he's got a gun!" Harold told the jury that as he turned, Albert fired the gun, and the bullet grazed him. He explained how he was able to wrestle the gun away from Albert:

> He hit me on the head with the gun—it checked me—then his arm was over my back with the gun and I got to his wrist and the gun dropped. I got a front headlock on him—I've done a little wrestling—then I kneed him in the chest. I hit him in the face and he stumbled against a chest of drawers. I grabbed him by the throat and then caught him by the hair. I bounced his head on the floor about four times and then dragged him around so I could call the doctor. Later a neighbor woman held him down by the hair.[4]

Betty took the witness stand and told the jury the events that took place when Albert arrived at their house. She told of Albert's plans to steal the family car and take her as a hostage. She said Albert told her he had never driven a car, but he assured her they would be safe. Betty said she continually asked to be allowed to use the telephone to call for help, but Albert told her he knew she "would trick him." Betty said her mother kept assuring Albert that they would not trick him.

Albert's uncle, William Atteberry, testified that Albert stole his firearm and his wristwatch weeks before the murder. He identified the weapon entered into evidence as the one he owned.

The jury heard from Earl Baccus, assistant fire chief, as to his findings upon arriving at the fire at the Crandalls' house. He spoke of finding Patricia's burned body. Warren Brusie testified that he removed the body and transported it to the funeral home.

All eyes were on Albert as he walked to the witness stand. The jury had just heard from District Attorney McPherson who read Albert's confession verbatim.

Albert immediately placed the blame on an eighteen-year-old named "Jack." The reason "Jack" killed Patricia, according to Albert, was that she rejected his advances. Albert refused to give "Jack's" last name. As for shooting Myrtle, Albert said it was an accident. He admitted stealing the German Luger pistol from his uncle, but said he thought the safety was on when he aimed the weapon at Myrtle. Hs then added: "I had my finger on the trigger and pulled the trigger. I don't know whether I was aiming it at her." When asked by the prosecution why he never mentioned "Jack" in his confession, Albert explained that "Jack" was an adult, and he did not want him to be executed.

The six men and six women who made up the jury deliberated for nine hours before returning a verdict of guilty of first-degree murder for Patricia and guilty of second-degree murder for Myrtle. They also found Albert guilty of attempted murder for Harold but rejected the two counts of assault with a deadly weapon with the intent to commit murder for Betty and Barbara.

Judge Delrup shocked everyone, including Albert, when he ordered Albert to begin treatment at the Mendocino State Hospital instead of being sent to San Quentin prison for life. This was the first case in California to consider mental health treatment instead of incarceration. Dr. Rappaport of the Mendocino State Hospital asked defense attorney Carr to draft a revision for the State Legislature so that future cases could be given the same consideration.

Instead of starting his freshman year at Chico Senior High School, Albert entered the Mendocino State Hospital. Five years later Albert was transferred to San Quentin prison. One year into his stay, he stabbed a fellow inmate eleven times. The inmate survived and Albert was placed in solitary confinement for a period of time.

17

The Tom Gray Gang

On April 5, 1922, the Bank of Arcadia was robbed. After learning that the bank had been robbed, deputies headed to Coyote Pass and searched fifty cars. The deputies were told someone fired a gun at the getaway car and it should have two bullet holes and blood on the backseat.

When the deputies stopped a car with a false license plate, they encountered four men. Two of the men had firearms. The deputies immediately noticed two empty money bags on the floorboard of the car. However, there was no evidence of the $10,000 in cash, the stolen money orders, or the negotiable bonds that the robbers left the bank with. There was no evidence that the car had been shot at.

Nevertheless, the four men were arrested and questioned at length at the jail. All of the men vehemently denied any wrongdoing. They explained they were never near the bank. The deputies were not satisfied and took the men to the bank, where the bank employees identified the men as the robbers.

The men were placed in separate jail cells in the Los Angeles County jail. One of the men died while incarcerated at the county jail. The other three men, Jose Hernandez, Broulio Galindo, and Salvadore Mendival, were sent to prison after being convicted of robbing the Bank of Arcadia.

Even with the men in prison, rumors persisted that the wrong men were convicted. Nearly two years passed when word came that there was a cover up and the men in prison were wrongfully convicted after being railroaded for the crime. The investigators believed the robbery was staged by the Tom Gray Gang and high-ranking officials were involved in planning the bank robbery and participated in the share of the stolen money.

Los Angeles Deputy Sheriff A. W. Fitzgerald announced there would be arrests for the men responsible for their part in the cover up of the robbery of the Bank of Arcadia. He expanded by saying the suspects were part of the Tom Gray Gang. At the top of the list was Frank J. Sullivan. They believed Frank was the person who planned the bank robbery and drove the getaway car.

The first suspect arrested was former Los Angeles Police Officer Hubert Kittle. He was charged with receiving stolen property. The crux of the investigation was the money orders that were stolen from the Bank of Arcadia and later cashed in Tijuana, Mexico. The owner of the store where the money orders were cashed testified before the grand jury that he cashed $1,200 of money orders for Hubert, who was with several friends at the time. At Hubert's arraignment, he pled not guilty. Superior Court Judge Sherik reduced Hubert's bail from $25,000 to $7,500. Hubert was released from the county jail after posting $2,500 in cash and $5,000 in bonds.

Deputy Sheriff Fitzgerald told reporters a young lady testified before a grand jury. She informed the grand jury she overheard the Tom Gray Gang planning to rob the Bank of Arcadia and later saw the proceeds from the bank robbery. The authorities allowed the woman to remain anonymous for her own safety.

Deputy Sheriff Fitzgerald said he had heard rumors that the Tom Gray Gang was responsible for the bank robbery and informed a "former high official" of the sheriff's office of this, but nothing came of it before the three men were convicted.

Los Angeles District Attorney Asa Keyes was outraged after learning of the cover up and announced: "This affair of officers framing three apparently innocent men will set back for ten years the enforcement of the law in Los Angeles." Los Angeles County Sheriff W. I. Traeger referred to the case as "the biggest blow-up in the history of Los Angeles."

The three men who were wrongfully convicted were pardoned by Governor Richardson and released from prison after serving almost two years.

The detectives soon learned Tom Gary had been convicted of armed robbery in Oregon twelve years prior to the Bank of Arcadia robbery. Tom served five years before escaping. He remained a free man for nearly seven years until he was captured shortly after the investigation into the bank robbery and returned to the Oregon State Penitentiary.

Although Hubert initially refused to talk, he later changed his mind and was interviewed for four hours about the bank robbery. Hubert later clarified with reporters his involvement with suspect D. J. MacGregor who was with him when he allegedly cashed the stolen money orders,

Hubert returned home after being questioned by the police. Rumors began to swell that the police planned to re-arrest Hubert. Before that could happen, Hubert took his own life by ingesting poison. The police spoke with his wife, Dot, who admitted Hubert had fired a gun the night before in their home. She emphasized she did not feel he was a threat to her or their two sons, ages five and seven. Dot did say he planned "to go out fighting if anyone tried to arrest him again." Within the Hubert's home, the police located two rifles, three pistols, a pint of nitroglycerine, 300 rounds of ammunition, and a large amount of cyanide that they described as being "enough to kill a hundred people."

Suspect Jack "Buck" O'Neill was arrested and quickly turned state's evidence. He was awaiting trial on another bank robbery that he alleged Jack Sullivan was involved with. He provided the prosecutors with inside information about the robbery of the Bank of Arcadia. He placed the blame for the robbery of the Bank of Arcadia squarely on Jack Sullivan and confirmed he drove the getaway car.

Two of the suspects, James Blanton and William O'Connor, proved to be difficult to locate. The two suspects were also wanted for the robbery of the Provident Loan Company in Los Angeles. The loss for that robbery totaled $200,000 in gems. They were also wanted for drug smuggling.

When the police finally caught up to James, he was dead on the living room floor of his apartment. The police believed his associates killed him as revenge for taking more than his share of the proceeds from the robbery of the Provident Loan Company. Their investigation revealed James turned over some of the stolen property to a person who was supposed to sell it and give the gang the money. The detectives believed after the property was sold, James robbed the person who sold the property and kept all of the money, instead of dividing it between the members of the gang.

Two months later, William was arrested in San Francisco after exchanging gunfire with the police. A team of detectives surrounded the building at 6th and Bryant Streets where William had been living under an assumed name. As soon as William figured out the police were outside his apartment, he attempted to go down the fire escape. When a detective fired his weapon, William went back inside the apartment all the while firing his gun in the direction of the detective. Once William was inside the apartment, the detectives fired their weapons through the closed door. William returned fire until he ran out of bullets, then declared: "I'm through boys, I've done the best I could. My right arms gone." William suffered a gunshot to his right arm, his side, and his neck.

Once William was in custody, he was identified as the person who robbed a home and got away with $5,000 in diamonds. He was also charged with other bank robberies. A trial was held, and he was sentenced to life imprisonment.

When the police arrived at William's apartment, they saw a female fleeing out the back of the building. They believed the female had eluded them in an automobile the previous night. It turned out the female was James' girlfriend, Eva Taylor. She was arrested when she arrived at the jail to visit William. She was questioned about her involvement in the robbery of the Houston-Gilmore Jewelry Company where $100,000 in gems was stolen. Eva was released and continued to deny that James was involved in any robberies.

After a lengthy investigation into the robbery of the Bank of Arcadia, the investigators closed their case. They believed with Tom and William serving life sentences, and James and Hubert deceased, the gang had been dismantled. Also, with the three men exonerated who were wrongfully convicted, they completed their work on the case.

18
The Bombing of the Los Angeles Times Building

At 1 a.m. on October 1, 1910, the employees at the *Los Angeles Times* were putting the finishing touches on the morning edition of the newspaper. Suddenly a huge blast shook the building, tearing the brick walls wide open. Within minutes, the gas lines next to the building exploded and the entire building became an inferno.

Emergency personnel rushed to the scene only to find a huge crater where the building had stood at the corner of First and Broadway Streets in Los Angeles since 1886. The building was part of what was known as "Ink Alley" due to the number of newspaper and magazine publishing houses that occupied the area.

The explosion was felt more than a mile away, and the windows and doors of nearby buildings were blown out. Spectators flooded the street as the police struggled to keep everyone away from the smoldering ruins. Looters took advantage of the open buildings in the vicinity.

The investigators on scene at the *Los Angeles Times* building were able to determine that dynamite had been used to blow up the building and, in turn, set the gas lines on fire creating an inferno.

Hours later detectives were called to the home of General Harrison Gray Otis on Wilshire Boulevard and Parkville Avenue. General Otis was the president of the Times-Mirror Company and the editor-in-chief of the *Los Angeles Times*. He was in Mexico when the *Los Angeles Times* building was dynamited. A caretaker at his house discovered a briefcase in the bushes and contacted the police. The detectives opened the briefcase and discovered twelve sticks of dynamite bound with wire and an alarm clock. The alarm clock was set to go off at the same time that the *Los Angeles Times* building was bombed. The alarm clock had been wound too tightly and failed to go off. The bomb did, however, go off when a detective dropped the briefcase once he realized what was in it. The detectives were able to run for safety when they heard a roar, moments before the bomb went off. No one was injured, but the landscaping suffered a great deal of damage.

Later that day, Felix Zechandelaar located a bomb wrapped in newspaper on the outside of his house. Felix was the secretary of the Los Angeles Merchants' and Manufacturers Association and had been vocal against unions. The bomb that had been placed under his daughter's window never detonated. Witnesses came forward with information that five men were seen loitering around the Zechandelaar's house on Garland Avenue earlier in the day.

The Los Angeles City Council authorized $25,000 for the investigation into those responsible for the bombings. They also authorized hiring forty additional police officers, ten sergeants, and one lieutenant. The new hires were selected based on the civil service eligibility list and began work immediately.

Early on in their investigation, the detectives were able to determine that labor unions were involved. The *Los Angeles Times* had refused to unionize and fought against unions for twenty years.

The managing editor of the *Los Angeles Times*, Harry Chandler, told the United Press:

> We have had hundreds of threatening letters from Union laborites during the past dozen years, but lately the threats that have come to us in anonymous letters have been more savage than any heretofore. We have grown used to these epistolary threats and so we have not paid much attention to them.
>
> There is not a shadow of a doubt that we were victims of dynamiters in the labor unions. They have simply executed their long-time threats. Their plan was to kill me. I am about always in my office between 11 p.m. and 2 a.m. I happened to be out of the office and building when the dynamite exploded. Thus my life was saved. The explosion occurred close to my private office and within twelve feet of my desk. My secretary, who was busy at my desk, was instantly killed.[1]

The union labor groups came out against the bombing and adamantly denied being involved. They blamed the explosion on ruptured gas lines. The city of Los Angeles cancelled a parade the unions were planning. They also put the naval militia on standby fearing there could be rioting in the streets between those in favor and those opposed to unions.

After days of searching for bodies, the police announced that of the 115 workers in the building at the time of the explosion and fire, twenty lost their lives. More than 100 workers were injured.

A fund was set up to assist the families of the deceased. Fundraisers were held, and people from all across the country sent cash ranging from one dollar to several hundred dollars. Within weeks, the fund totaled $75,000. The money was distributed to the widows and children of those who died in the explosion and fire.

On Christmas Day 1910, The Llellewyn Iron Works in Los Angeles was dynamited. No one was in the building at the time of the explosion.

The detectives were able to determine that 500 pounds of 80 percent nitro powder had been placed aboard a boat bearing the name *Peerless* shortly before the *Los Angeles Times* building was bombed. The detectives traveled to the Giant Powder Company in San Francisco in an attempt to locate the man who sold the dynamite and the person(s) who purchased it. They were able to determine who purchased the dynamite and where it was sent after leaving San Francisco.

After a six-month investigation, John McNamara was arrested for his part in the bombing of the *Los Angeles Times* building. John was the international secretary of the Bridge and Structural Iron Workers of America based in Indianapolis, Indiana.

A search warrant was executed at the headquarters of the Bridge and Structural Iron Workers in Indianapolis. The police located sixty-four sticks of dynamite weighing 60 pounds, 200 hundred feet of fuse, 500 dynamite caps, one dozen alarm clocks, and a leather case that could hold a 10-pound can of nitroglycerine.

A search of a barn just outside of Indianapolis that John had rented revealed two quarts of nitroglycerine and seventeen sticks of dynamite. The police believed John and his associates were planning to blow up four railroad bridges and a new railroad terminal in Detroit, Michigan.

John's brother, James, was arrested for his part in bombing the *Los Angeles Times* building. He adamantly denied any involvement. The police believed the McNamara brothers were responsible for more than a dozen bombings throughout the United States.

Ortie McManigal was arrested and charged with the bombing of the Llellewyn Iron Works. Detectives located apparatus to make clocks in a workshop on his property that they believed were used in the bombings.

Prior to being sent back to California, Ortie and James spent a week at Detective William Reed's home in Chicago. James refused to answer any questions and continued to deny any involvement with the bombing of the *Los Angeles Times* building. Ortie, on the other hand, confessed over four hours in front of a stenographer and detectives. He told the detectives he participated in bombing jobs in Toledo, Ohio; Cleveland, Ohio; Kansas City, Missouri; Peoria, Illinois; Milwaukee, Wisconsin; and Springfield, Massachusetts. He placed the blame for all of the bombings on the McNamara brothers.

In answering the media's questions about this unorthodox custody arrangement, Chief of Detectives Wood responded:

> Both McNamara and McManigal were kept for a week at Reed's home and treated as guests, not prisoners. We did not need to administer any third degree. McManigal was already willing to tell all. He was not mistreated or bulldozed. McManigal had a stenographer for more than a week and frequently consulted memorandum books and papers. Detectives Reed and Bendiger, acting for William J. Burns, are taking the men arrested to the Pacific Coast.[2]

It was announced that attorney Charles Darrow would represent the McNamara brothers. He received $100 per day from the labor unions to represent the brothers. The trial opened fourteen months after the bombing and fire of the *Los Angeles Times* building.

The jury heard Ortie's confession about bombing jobs spread across the United States. Ortie took the witness stand and testified against John and James while explaining his own involvement. He stressed that the brothers ordered each of the bombing jobs and that he never received payment for a bombing job until John examined the aftermath of the bombing.

The trial had barely gotten underway when John and James changed their not guilty pleas to guilty. The prosecution presented evidence that there had been jury tampering by trying to bribe a few of the jurors for voting to acquit the McNamaras. That coupled with Ortie's confession led to a change of heart, and the brothers pled guilty.

Defense attorney Clarence Darrow told reporters: "It was a hard struggle to bring this about, but it was the best thing that could have happened. I did the best I could."

John received a sentence of fifteen years to be served at San Quentin prison. James received a life imprisonment sentence. Ortie served more than a year in jail before being released and moving to Great Britain.

Thirty-eight other workers of the International Association of Bridge and Structural Iron Workers and other labor members were found guilty in federal court after a federal jury heard from 500 witnesses. They men were sent to Leavenworth for varying lengths of time.

John served nine years at San Quentin prison for his part in the bombing. James died at San Quentin prison after serving nearly thirty years between Folsom and San Quentin prisons.

19

A Pasadena Murder Mystery

In the early morning hours of December 13, 1933, Harold Fox was delivering milk in Pasadena when he came across a body lying in the driveway of the Scottish Rite Cathedral. The police arrived and discovered Dr. Leonard Siever, age forty-four, dead from two gunshot wounds.

Leonard was a dentist in Pasadena and was well known in the community. Pasadena police chief of detectives told the media: "I am convinced the motive for this killing was revenge. A note was found on the body and the wounds indicate that someone had a great grudge against him."

One of the notes read: "11:30 Tuesday Rockwell." They were unable to determine if Leonard was meeting someone at 11:30 the night he was murdered or if the note had some other meaning. There was another note in his pocket, but the detectives determined that note was in regards to Leonard trading his dental services for French lessons. After further investigation, the detectives determined the French teacher was not involved.

Although Leonard's wallet and watch were missing, the detectives believed that was staged to make it appear that it was a robbery. They learned the location of Leonard's vehicle was in close proximity to his office and he frequently parked there. Leonard's briefcase was untouched, and he still had the key to the vehicle.

The autopsy revealed Leonard had been shot in the head and in the chest. The detectives believed that Leonard was shot behind his left ear as he approached his car and then shot through the chest at close range as he lay on the ground.

The caretaker for the cathedral did not see anyone or hear any gunshots prior to the body being discovered. However, he attributed this to the weather the night of the murder, which was blustery with heavy rain.

In checking with Leonard's friends, the detectives learned he rented a room in Dr. Francis Weston's house in Pasadena. Leonard was active in many cultural circles in Pasadena, Los Angeles, and Beverly Hills. He was not married and did not have any relatives nearby. Leonard's sister flew from Connecticut to assist with the investigation, but she was unable to furnish the police with any answers.

Further checking revealed Leonard was dating a woman and was scheduled to take her to a friend's house for dinner the night his body was discovered. She was interviewed at length, but the police came away without any answers.

The investigation led to a trunk Leonard kept in his room. Within the trunk were many letters written by females he had dated at one time. None of the letters offered the detectives any answers. One woman who was briefly engaged to Leonard, told the police Leonard once told her he had a "purple secret," but she did not have any further information. Other witnesses said Leonard kept his personal life very private.

The detectives interviewed numerous people, but no one was able to shed any light on the case. They did learn that Leonard wrote out a promissory note for $8,500 to a physician in Pasadena. The detectives were not able to determine why Leonard needed that much money. They were not able to determine if he had a large gambling debt, if he was being blackmailed, or if it was a purchase for his business.

The police were hopeful that Leonard's safety deposit box would hold some clues. After examining the safety deposit box, they came away empty handed.

The detectives sent teletypes nationwide asking for assistance locating Leonard's watch.

The watch did turn up, but not in the way the police expected. The woman Leonard had been dating received an envelope with the watch and a ransom note demanding $5,000. In exchange for the $5,000, the note writer promised to turn over the murder weapon. The writer explained he had seen the murderer bury the weapon and he retrieved it. Handwriting experts were not able to provide any clues as to who wrote the note. The police had Leonard's girlfriend place an ad in the local newspaper asking for additional information, but none was forthcoming.

The police received a letter from a female inmate who was serving time for murdering her husband. She claimed that her husband killed Leonard in a jealous rage. The investigators were able to determine that the inmate and Leonard were in Palm Springs at the same time and the inmate visited Pasadena, but they were never able to tie the inmate and Leonard together.

A private investigator by the name of Harry Karsch provided the investigators Leonard's diary and other personal papers he claimed he took out of Leonard's office the day his body was discovered. In the diary was a notation on the day Leonard was murdered, that read, "Date with L.B. at 5:30. Don't know what I'm going to do." The detectives were never able to determine who L.B. was.

The private investigator also told the detectives a man gave him the murder weapon and asked him to take it to Mexico and hide it. The investigators retrieved a gun from law enforcement in Tijuana that the private investigator said was the firearm used to murder Leonard. The ballistics test was inconclusive due to the poor condition of the firearm.

The calendar clicked over to 1934 without any arrests, and it has done so every year since then.

20

The Thirty Strong Gang

At noon on October 13, 1920, four armed men walked into the Alameda County Bank of Alvarado (now Union City) and demanded all of the money in the bank. The president of the bank, August May, attempted to knock the gun out of one of the robber's hands but was shot twice in the shoulder by one of the other robbers. The employees handed over $23,428 and the robbers ran to their getaway car that they had stolen minutes before and drove off before the police were notified.

August was taken to Merritt Hospital where he underwent surgery and remained in critical care for days before he rallied and was released.

Law enforcement from Alameda, Oakland, and Berkeley spread out in search of the getaway car and the robbers. The following day the car was located in West Oakland, but there was no sign of the bank robbers.

The police were still working on the bank robbery case when they were called out to a number of crimes at the beginning of 1921.

On January 29, 1921, the Bradford Market on Market Street in Oakland was held up at night by two men who got away with $200 in coins.

The Hotel Harrison located at 14th and Harrison Streets in Oakland was held up by two men at the end of January 1921. The men stole the employee's automatic revolver and $55.

At the beginning of February 1921, the Hotel Vernon was held up by two men who demanded the $60 that was in the cash drawer.

A garage in Concord was burglarized resulting in the loss of several thousand dollars' worth of merchandise.

A garage in Pleasanton was burglarized with a loss of $2,500 worth of goods stolen.

The Ralph and Scribner Store in Alavadero was burglarized. The burglars got away with several thousand dollars' worth of merchandise.

At the beginning of February 1921, San Francisco Police Officer John Trainer was shot while confronting three men who were trying to break into a drugstore at Laguna and McAllister Streets in San Francisco. One of the three men was captured, but the other two got away. Officer Trainer was able to fire his weapon and one of the suspects who got away was struck by the bullet. Officer Trainer recovered from his injuries.

As the detectives began trying to link the cases to suspects, they took another look at a liquor store robbery that occurred three weeks before the bank robbery. In that case, San Francisco Police Officer James W. Horton was killed in the line of duty when he was shot multiple times by the robbers.

There were other unsolved burglaries, robberies, and stolen cars in Alameda County during that time frame. There were reports of men driving at night and being forced to stop their cars and being robbed. People walking in Oakland and San Francisco reported being mugged and assaulted.

The detectives pieced together that the bank robbery suspects were part of the Thirty Strong Gang that had terrorized Oakland and San Francisco for months. Additional information about the Thirty Strong Gang was provided by a man after the police arrested him for a burglary.

Alameda County Sheriff Frank Barnet, Detective George Helms, and deputies Joseph Soares and John Collier worked with Alameda County District Attorney Erza Decoto. They enlisted the help of the San Francisco Police Department and the Oakland Police Department to takedown the Thirty Strong Gang.

The group of law enforcement spent weeks working undercover watching a group of men who they believed were responsible for the crimes. On one particular night, they observed the group of suspects leave a house on 19th Street in Oakland and walk downtown where they stole a vehicle.

On another night the group of law enforcement watched as four of the suspects stole a vehicle parked in front of the Hotel Oakland. They followed the vehicle until it returned to the house on 19th Street. At that time, twelve law enforcement officers from the Oakland Police Department surrounded the house. A contingent of officers, deputies, and detectives entered the house at 1 a.m. and took the suspects into custody. The suspects were armed with firearms, brass knuckles, and flashlights when law enforcement stormed the house.

Three hours later, additional law enforcement raided a house on 14th and Peralta Streets in Oakland. A short time later, a house on Chestnut Street in Alameda was raided by law enforcement. At all three locations, law enforcement seized an arsenal of weapons and ammunition, and items they believed were stolen from houses, stores, and garages in Alameda County. They also found a letter written by Prescott Rea referring to the attempted burglary at the drugstore where Officer Trainer was shot. The letter read, in part: "The cop is getting better and Felmming [sic] will pull out all right. It was a narrow escape."

The suspects who were arrested were Ralph Jones, Frank Strickland, William Kirk, Prescott Rea and his wife, Ruth, Eddie "Boston" Lenihan, Jack Beebe, Clarence Dye, Arthur Floyd, Larry Fitzgerald, John and Gladys Fleming, and John A. Sullivan.

William "Little Goog" Rossi was arrested in Iowa and Thomas "Lefty" Foley were arrested in Minnesota. "Lefty" was preparing to purchase a San Francisco newspaper when he was arrested. The police located newspaper clippings related to the Thirty Strong Gang in his pocket when they arrested him. He denied his true identity, but his fingerprints gave him away.

When William was interviewed after being arrested, he explained he and Gladys had two children together. He expanded by saying he previously worked as a road construction foreman in Ukiah. It was there that he met John Flemming, who was assigned to work on the highway as part of an honor program for a prison program where John was incarcerated. William said shortly after that, he and Gladys moved to Oakland. He recalled Gladys wrote a letter to John suggesting he move to Oakland when he was released from prison. He said it was not long after that John arrived in Oakland and Gladys allowed John and his associates to stay with them. He recalled numerous times the group would leave the house heavily armed with firearms and return with a cache of money and/or stolen goods. William admitted there was one day when he returned home from working in a shipyard and found Gladys and the men counting out the proceeds from a bank robbery. William explained that he and Gladys were divorced in November 1920, and she married John on Christmas night 1920.

William told the police that a man he knew by the name of "Lefty" appeared at their house after being shot by Officer Trainer. He said Gladys provided aid to the gunshot wound and kept him in the attic. William explained that when "Lefty" was in the attic, George Boyd and two of his friends came to the house.

The police knew that George, along with Terrance Fitts and Charles Valento, had been lynched in Santa Rosa by a group of angry citizens two months before. The three men were part of the "Howard Street Vice Gang" of San Francisco, which was an extension of the Thirty Strong Gang.

On Thanksgiving morning 1920, the police received a phone call saying two women were being held in a shack on Howard Street. The police arrived and located two women who said they attended a dance the night before and had been lured into an automobile by a group of men. They were taken to the shack and raped. The only men in the shack when the police arrived were Edward Kruvosky and Allen McDonnell. They were arrested and booked into the Santa Rosa jail.

Days later, two additional members of the Howard Street Vice Gang were arrested after a foot chase over the roofs of several buildings in Santa Rosa. Edmond "Spud" Murphy and Jim Carey were lodged at the Santa Rosa jail.

On December 5, 1920, Sonoma County Sheriff James Petray, San Francisco Police Officer Katherine O'Connor, Detective Lester Dorman, and Detective Sergeant Miles Jackson went to Santa Rosa to arrest Charles Valento, a member of the Howard Street Vice Gang. Other police officers surrounded the house.

At the house they located Charles, Terrance Fitts, and George Boyd. As they prepared to take the three men into custody, George suddenly opened fire, killing

Sheriff Petray, Detective Dorman, and Detective Sergeant Jackson. The law enforcement officers surrounding the house rushed in and took the three men into custody and booked them into the Santa Rosa jail.

George admitted he was the one who fired the weapon. It was determined that the firearm belonged to Charles and Terrance provided the ammunition. The district attorney used this information to charge all three men with first-degree murder. All three men were indicted by the grand jury.

An angry crowd of an estimated 2,000 people stood outside the jail and threatened to kill the three men who murdered the law enforcement authorities. The jail staff was able to keep things calm but five days later a group of vigilantes stormed the jail, pushed aside the jail staff and grabbed the master key to the jail cells. They opened the individual cell doors holding Terrance, George, and Charles. The three men were taken to the Santa Rosa cemetery and lynched.

The following day, huge crowds waited in line at the morgue to view the bodies. Throughout downtown Santa Rosa, crowds gathered to talk about the lynching.

A coroner's jury exonerated the jail staff. They ruled:

> Terrance Fitts, George Boyd and Charles Valento came to their death by being hanged from the neck by a lynching crowd of unknown persons, who stormed the county jail, overpowering the peace officer, and forcibly removed them for this purpose.
>
> We exonerate the sheriff and his deputies from any blame in connection herewith.[1]

Cities and towns throughout California cracked down on vice operations after learning of the murders of Sheriff Petray, Detective Dorman, and Detective Sergeant Jackson. The Santa Rosa City Council voted 4–1 to add ten more police officers to the Santa Rosa Police Department.

In Oakland, the commissioner of public health and safety ordered that all businesses with any "gang" affiliations be shut down. He was concerned that gang members that were run out of San Francisco would migrate to Oakland.

The detectives learned the planning for the robbery of the Alameda County Bank took place at the Howard Street shack, and that Charles Valente received a portion of the stolen currency for providing a place for them to plan the crime. They determined John A. Sullivan was the "mastermind" behind the bank robbery. The others involved were Jack Beebe, William "Little Goog" Rossi, "Lefty" Foley, and Larry Fitzgerald. All of the men involved in the bank robbery were convicted and sent to San Quentin prison.

Eddie Lenehan and Ralph Jones were responsible for robbing the hotels and were sent to Folsom prison. Frank Strickland was given two years' probation and sent to the county hospital after a doctor testified that Frank only had a short time to live.

John Fleming was sent to prison after being convicted of assault to murder for the attempted robbery of the drug store in San Francisco where Officer John Trainor was wounded after John shot him.

Edmond Murphy, Allen McDonald, James Carey, and Edward Kruvosky received sentences ranging from one to fifty years in prison.

William Kirk and Prescott Rea turned state's evidence in exchange for lesser prison sentences. Gladys received five years probation after pleading guilty to knowingly receiving stolen property. Prescott Rea also pled guilty to receiving stolen property and the charges were dropped against his wife, Ruth.

Five years after the takedown of the Thirty Strong Gang, police responded to an apartment on Green Street in San Francisco. They had received an anonymous phone call suggesting they "inspect" the apartment. Eugene Bowen lay dead on the bedroom floor with multiple gunshots to his head and body. His girlfriend, Dorothy Wilson, was seriously wounded from gunshots to her side and her arm. She told the police a man she knew as "Clyde" and another man rang her doorbell and demanded to be let into the apartment. She said she refused to let them in, but they forced their way inside and began shooting. The police noticed several bullet holes in the walls of the apartment. The police knew "Clyde" as Clyde Hilliard, the man they referred to as "the crook without a friend." They also knew Gladys had been Eugene's girlfriend until she began a relationship with Clyde. The police began looking for Clyde.

When the police did locate Clyde, he was lying dead from multiple gunshots wounds in San Francisco. Gladys was with him, and she, too, had been shot, but refused to identify the assailant. She recovered from her wounds after two surgeries.

Only a portion of the $23,428 stolen during the bank robbery was recovered.

Endnotes

Chapter 1
1 *Oakland Tribune*, June 20, 1929, p. 2.
2 *The San Francisco Examiner*, November 28, 1943, p. 10.
3 *Ibid.*
4 *The Sacramento Bee*, April 25, 1952, p. 8.

Chapter 2
1 *Chicago Tribune*, December 1, 1916, p. 13.
2 *St. Louis Post-Dispatch*, November 5, 1933, p. 56.

Chapter 3
1 *The Hanford Sentinel*, December 19, 1927, p. 5.
2 *Morning Tribune*, December 21, 1927, p. 1.
3 *Visalia Daily Times*, December 22, 1927, p. 4.
4 *Ibid.*
5 *Ibid.*
6 *Imperial Valley Press*, December 23, 1927, p. 1.
7 *Ibid.*
8 *Ibid.*
9 *Ibid.*
10 *Morning Tribune*, December 28, 1927, p. 1.
11 *The Hanford Sentinel*, February 7, 1928, p. 8.
12 *The San Francisco Examiner*, February 10, 1928, p. 2.
13 *Ibid.*

Chapter 4
1 *The San Francisco Examiner*, June 12, 1931, p. 3.
2 *Oakland Tribune*, May 4, 1932, p. 1.
3 *The San Francisco Examiner*, May 7, 1932, p. 4.
4 *The San Francisco Examiner*, June 5, 1932, p. 3.
5 *The Press Democrat*, June 8, 1932, p. 2.
6 *The San Francisco Examiner*, June 22, 1932, p. 3.
7 *The San Francisco Examiner*, August 29, 1932, p. 5.
8 *The San Francisco Examiner*, September 10, 1932, p. 2.
9 *The San Francisco Examiner*, September 21, 1932, p. 1.

10 *Santa Cruz Sentinel*, November 17, 1932, p. 1.
11 *The Sacramento Bee*, October 8, 1932, p. 1.
12 *Ibid.*
13 *The San Francisco Examiner*, November 20, 1934, p. 19.
14 *Ibid.*

Chapter 5
1 *Los Angeles Evening Post-Record*, September 9, 1933, p. 2.
2 *The Californian Erskine Johnson*, November 11, 1933, p. 7.
3 *The Pomona Progress Bulletin*, November 6, 1933, p. 9.
4 *Los Angeles Evening Post-Record*, December 6, 1933, p. 2.
5 *Ibid.*

Chapter 6
1 *Monrovia News-Post*, September 30, 1940, p. 1.
2 *Los Angeles Evening Citizen News*, June 12, 1947, p. 5.

Chapter 7
1 *The Los Angeles Times*, March 27, 1906, p. 6.
2 *Ibid.*
3 *Ibid.*
4 *The San Francisco Examiner*, June 22, 1906, p. 3.

Chapter 8
1 *The Los Angeles Times*, December 20, 1935, p. 9.

Chapter 9
1 *The San Bernardino County Sun*, January 27, 1946, p. 1.
2 *The San Bernardino County Sun*, January 28, 1946, p. 1–2.

Chapter 10
1 *The Los Angeles Times*, May 8, 1945, p. 11.

Chapter 11
1 *Los Angeles Evening Post-Record*, July 20, 1923, p. 2.
2 *Ibid.*
3 *Ibid.*
4 *The Pasadena Post*, June 18, 1930, p. 1–2.

Chapter 12
1 *Santa Ana Register*, August 8, 1925, p. 1.
2 *The Press Democrat*, August 4, 1925, p. 6.

Chapter 13
1 *Miles City Star*, July 26, 1931, p. 1.
2 *The San Bernardino County Sun*, October 10, 1936, p. 10.
3 *The Los Angeles Times*, January 30, 1947, p. 2.
4 *The Los Angeles Times*, July 27, 1947, p. 3.

Chapter 14
1 *The San Francisco Examiner*, May 28, 1940, p. 1.
2 *The San Francisco Examiner*, May 28, 1940, p. 20.
3 *Ibid*.
4 *The San Francisco Examiner*, July 11, 1940, p. 11.

Chapter 15
1 *Herald and Review*, August 21, 1934, p. 8.
2 *Des Moines Tribune*, February 13, 1939, p. 3.
3 *The Los Angeles Times*, May 4, 1946, p. 3.
4 *The San Francisco Examiner*, December 1, 1948, p. 4.

Chapter 16
1 *Enterprise Record*, Paul Thompson, July 18, 1946, p. 6.
2 *Ibid*.
3 *Enterprise Record*, July 20, 1946, p. 1.
4 *Oroville Mercury Register*, February 26, 1947, p. 8.

Chapter 18
1 *The Pomona Daily Review*, October 1, 1910, p. 1.
2 *The Seattle Star*, April 24, 1911, p. 1.

Chapter 20
1 *The Chico Enterprise Record*, December 11, 1920, p. 1.

Bibliography

Chicago Tribune, December 1, 1916, p. 13.
Des Moines Tribune, February 13, 1939, p. 3.
Herald and Review, August 21, 1934, p. 8.
Imperial Valley Press, December 23, 1927, p. 1.
Los Angeles Evening Citizen News, June 12, 1947, p. 5.
Los Angeles Evening Post-Record, December 6, 1933, p. 2.
Los Angeles Evening Post-Record, July 20, 1923, p. 2.
Los Angeles Evening Post-Record, September 9, 1933, p. 2.
Miles City Star, July 26, 1931, p. 1.
Monrovia News-Post, September 30, 1940, p. 1.
Morning Tribune, December 21, 1927, p. 1.
Morning Tribune, December 28, 1927, p. 1.
Oakland Tribune, June 20, 1929, p. 2.
Oakland Tribune, May 4, 1932, p. 1.
Oroville Mercury Register, February 26, 1947, p. 8.
Santa Ana Register, August 8, 1925, p. 1.
Santa Cruz Sentinel, November 17, 1932, p. 1.
St. Louis Post-Dispatch, November 5, 1933, p. 56.
The Californian Erskine Johnson, November 11, 1933, p. 7.
The Chico Enterprise Record, December 11, 1920, p. 1.
The Chico Enterprise Record, July 20, 1946, p. 1.
The Chico Enterprise Record, Paul Thompson, July 18, 1946, p. 6.
The Hanford Sentinel, December 19, 1927, p. 5.
The Hanford Sentinel, February 7, 1928, p. 8.
The Los Angeles Times, January 30, 1947, p. 2.
The Los Angeles Times, July 27, 1947, p. 3.
The Los Angeles Times, March 27, 1906, p. 6.
The Los Angeles Times, May 4, 1946, p. 3.
The Los Angeles Times, May 8, 1945, p. 11.
The Pasadena Post, June 18, 1930, p. 1–2.
The Pomona Daily Review, October 1, 1910, p. 1.
The Pomona Progress Bulletin, November 6, 1933, p. 9.
The Press Democrat, August 4, 1925, p. 6.
The Press Democrat, June 8, 1932, p. 2.
The Sacramento Bee, April 25, 1952, p. 8.

The Sacramento Bee, October 8, 1932, p. 1.
The San Bernardino County Sun, January 27, 1946, p. 1.
The San Bernardino County Sun, January 28, 1946, p. 1–2.
The San Bernardino County Sun, October 10, 1936, p. 10.
The San Francisco Examiner, August 29, 1932, p. 5.
The San Francisco Examiner, December 1, 1948, p. 4.
The San Francisco Examiner, February 10, 1928, p. 2.
The San Francisco Examiner, July 11, 1940, p. 11.
The San Francisco Examiner, June 12, 1931, p. 3.
The San Francisco Examiner, June 22, 1906, p. 3.
The San Francisco Examiner, June 22, 1932, p. 3.
The San Francisco Examiner, June 5, 1932, p. 3.
The San Francisco Examiner, May 28, 1940, p. 1.
The San Francisco Examiner, May 28, 1940, p. 20.
The San Francisco Examiner, May 7, 1932, p. 4.
The San Francisco Examiner, November 20, 1934, p. 19.
The San Francisco Examiner, November 28, 1943, p. 10.
The San Francisco Examiner, September 10, 1932, p. 2.
The San Francisco Examiner, September 21, 1932, p. 1.
The Seattle Star, April 24, 1911, p. 1.
Visalia Daily Times, December 22, 1927, p. 4.